WHITEPARIS

100 YEARS OF
AN ENGLISH VILLAGE

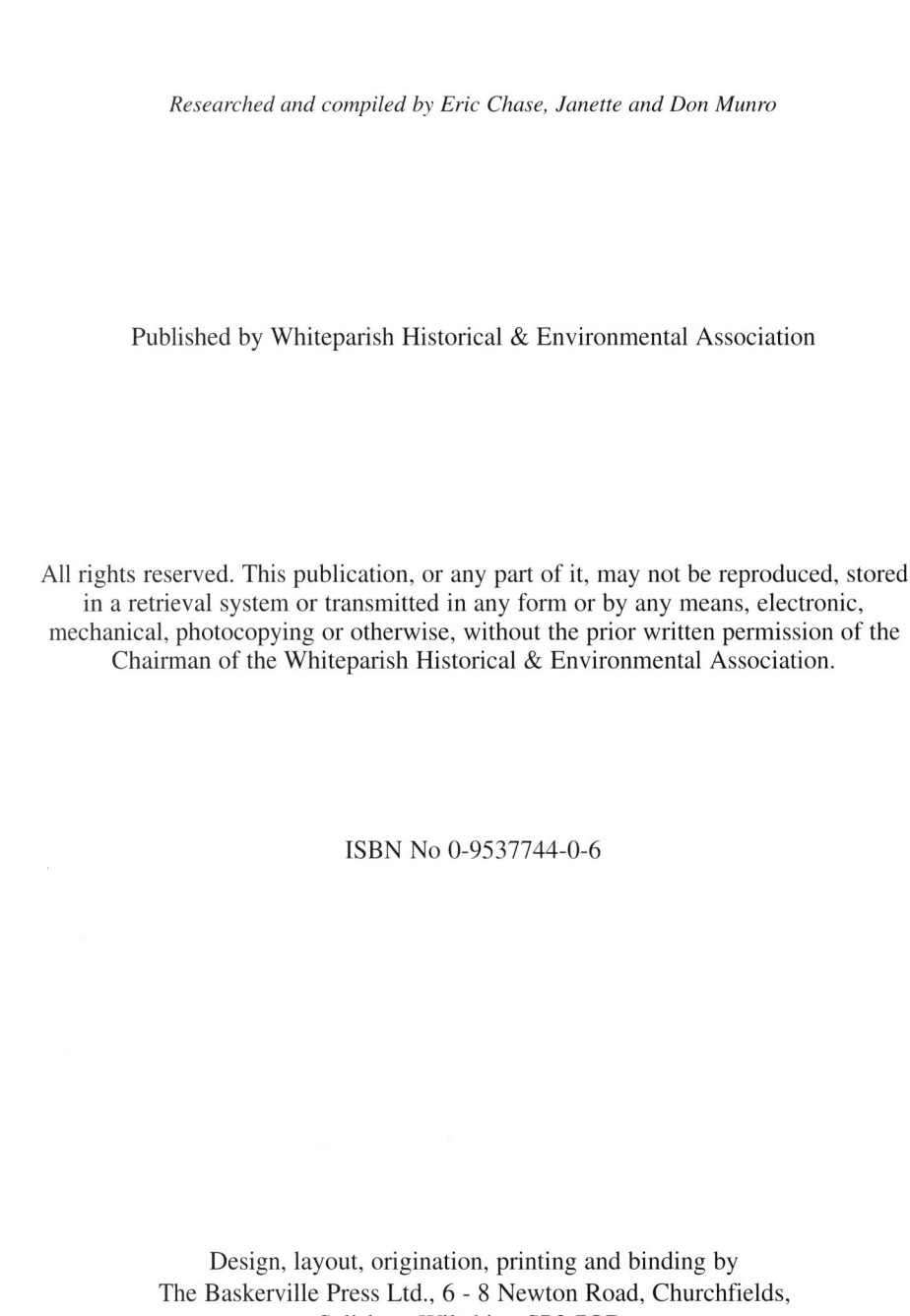

Researched and compiled by Eric Chase, Janette and Don Munro

Published by Whiteparish Historical & Environmental Association

ISBN No 0-9537744-0-6

Design, layout, origination, printing and binding by
The Baskerville Press Ltd., 6 - 8 Newton Road, Churchfields,
Salisbury,Wiltshire, SP2 7QB.

WHITEPARISH

100 YEARS OF
AN ENGLISH VILLAGE

as told by people of the village

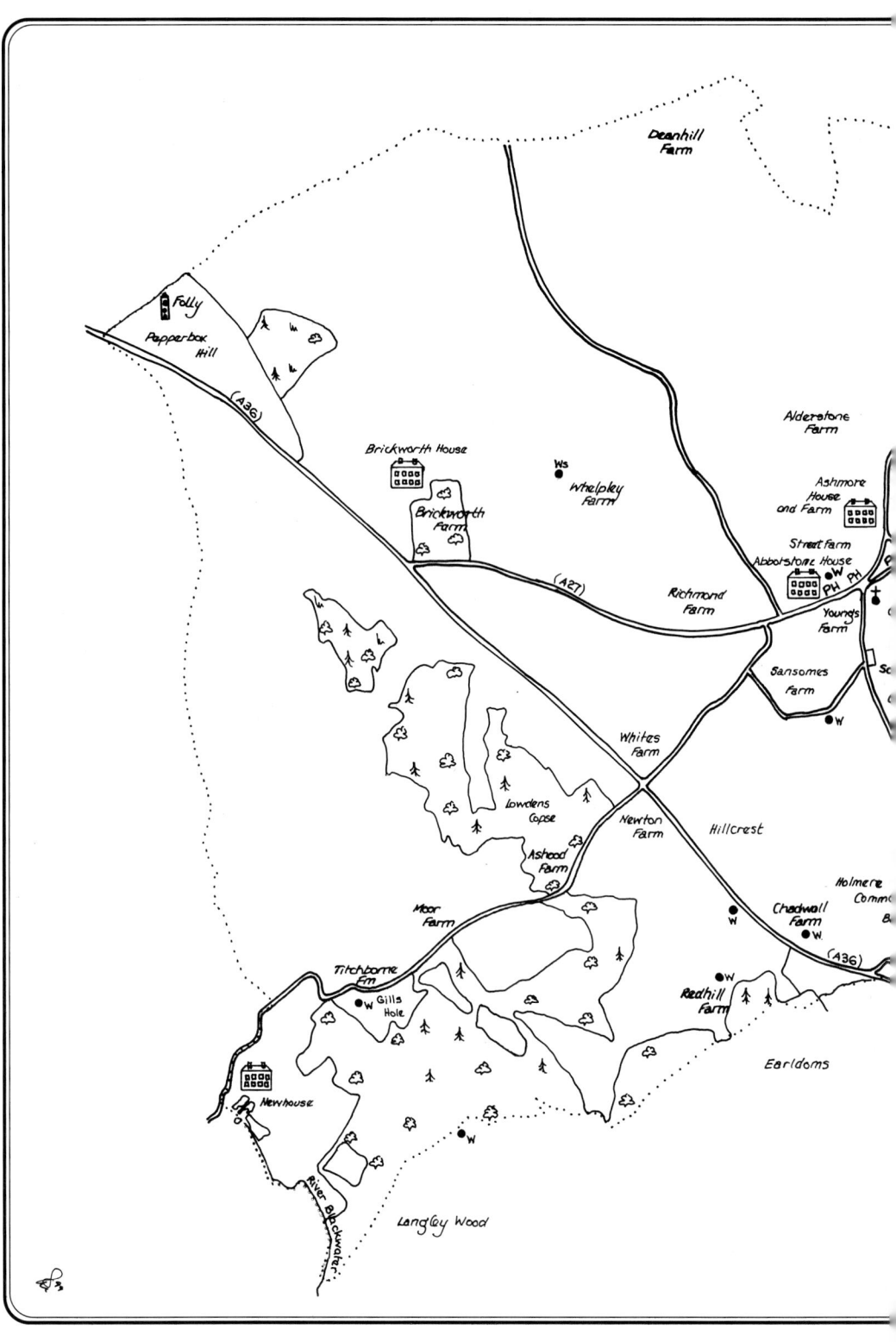

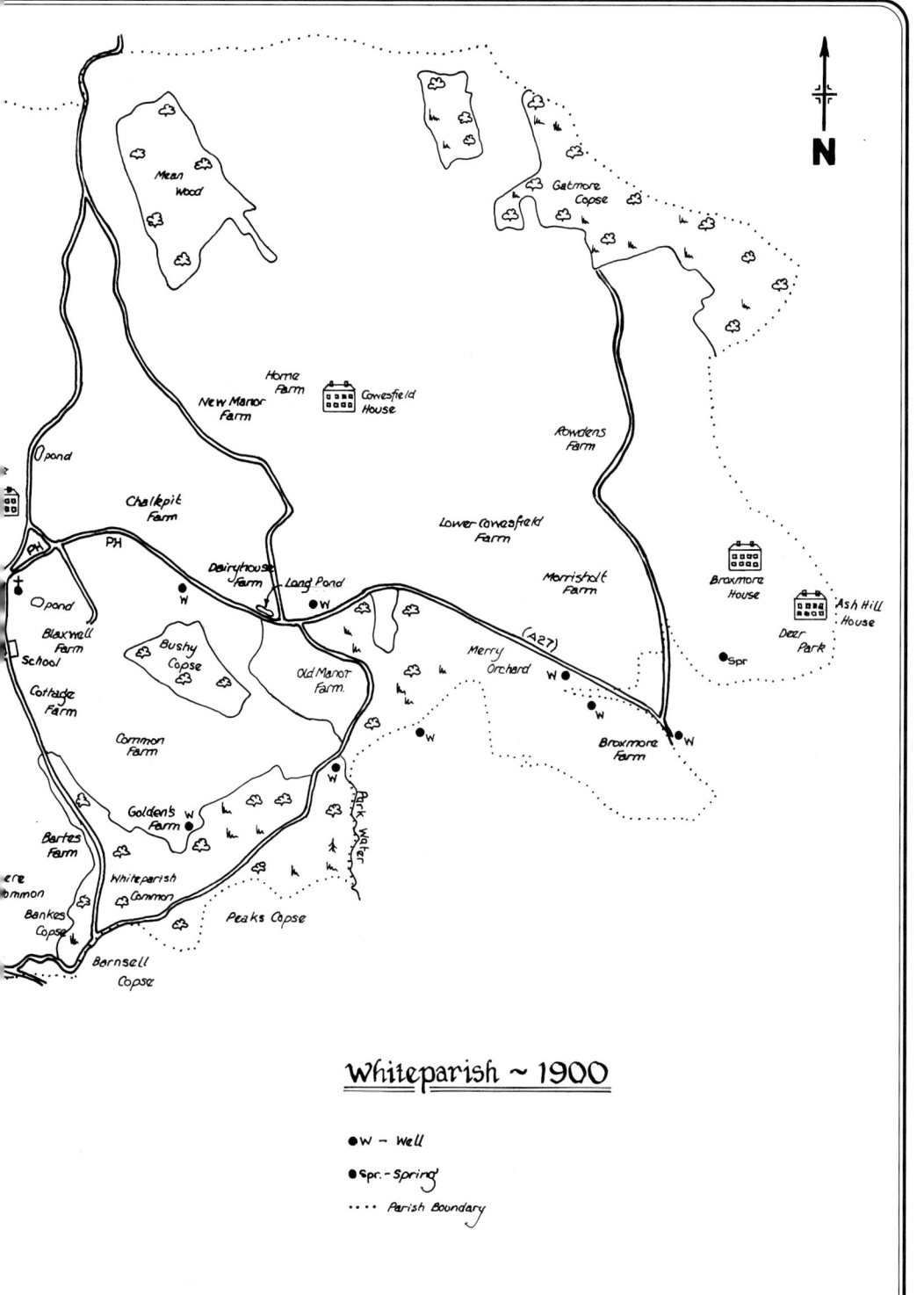

Whiteparish ~ 1900

●w – Well

●Spr. – Spring

.... Parish Boundary

Mean Wood

Gatmore Copse

Horne Farm

New Manor Farm

Cowesfield House

Rowdens Farm

O pond

Chalkpit Farm

Lower Cowesfield Farm

PH

PH

Dairyhouse Farm

Long Pond

W

Morrisholt Farm

Broxmore House

Ash Hill House

O pond

W

Blaxwell Farm School

Bushy Copse

Old Manor Farm

Merry Orchard

(A27)

W

Deer Park

●Spr

Cottage Farm

W

W

Broxmore Farm

W

Common Farm

W

W

Golden's Farm

W

Bartes Farm

Whiteparish Common

Park Water

ere Common

Bankes Copse

Peaks Copse

Barnsell Copse

LIST OF CONTENTS

CONTENTS

CHAPTER 1

INTRODUCTION

Why, you may ask, write a book that only sets out the history of the Parish for just 100 years?

It was our considered opinion, that if we went back for 1000 years we could not possibly compress the entire story into one book. In any case much of the pre 1900 history has been recorded by others and can be read elsewhere.

The last one hundred years of this millennium contains much that we can relate to, through older relations or those who have lived almost all their lives within its bounds. We felt that this history would be of great interest to those, now far too young to understand, but in twenty to fifty years would be able to read a very complete picture of the life that spawned them.

We hope that what we have written will give a flavour of the century, a century that went through one of the most turbulent periods of the world and one that leapt as never before into a new technological era.

'Villagers photographed outside two of the village pubs 'Kings Head' and 'Fountain Inn'1999.

We have attempted to write about each section that makes up village life. However this is not always easy, and at times the history intermingles.

The information in this book has been gleaned from many sources, memories of senior and junior parishioners, scrapbooks, old magazines and parish records that are kept at the Wiltshire Archives in Trowbridge. We do not pretend that all we have recorded is 100% correct, we hope it is, but should anyone find that they can dispute our facts please let us know! We hope that you enjoy reading it.

CHAPTER 2

NATURAL HISTORY
OF WHITEPARISH

- A review of the past century -

Our parish has a variety of habitats and wildlife, due in no small part to its complex underlying geology. There are chalk grasslands in the northern parts, wet meadows on the more central clays and extensive tracts of woodland not only on the sands and gravels to the south but also on both chalk and clay soils. This richness and diversity is reflected in the designation by English Nature of two large Sites of Special Scientific Interest (SSSIs) within the parish.

In geological terms, Whiteparish is tucked under the rim of the Hampshire Basin. The rim is composed of chalk, which underlies Dean Hill. Overlying the chalk, and therefore tending to `fill the basin` are the younger deposits: London Clay and sands and gravels. Clay soils are typical of the central and southerly parts of the village whilst a band of sand can be found in Dean Lane, in The Street and in areas further south such as Earldoms.

The first edition of the 6" Ordnance Survey map (surveyed 1872) shows that the area of woodland within the parish has changed little over the intervening years. Some small sections to the north have been clear felled and ploughed and are now used for arable farming. The wetter and / or less fertile soils to the south have proved to be less attractive for cultivation and the major threat to the woodland in these areas has been the conversion to commercial conifer plantations.

Wooded Commons. In the south an almost continuous tract of woodland extends from Cowesfield in the east to Earldoms in the west. Within this complex lies Whiteparish and Holmere Commons, ancient woodland sites which are now an SSSI, originally designated in 1965 and modified in 1987. There is evidence (Taylor 1967) that this area was wooded in Saxon times. Traditionally these commons were managed as wood pasture and until about fifty years ago they were grazed. Rights of Common still exist over parts of the area although they are no longer exercised. It is possible to deduce the nature of their use by reference to the parish tithe map and register (1840) and to a map of Mr. Bristow`s holdings (Whiteparish Particular Survey 1801) which show that tithes collected from these areas related to grazing fees rather than to wood collection. As in parts of the New Forest today, this type of management would have produced widely spaced mature trees with little shrub, saplings or flowers at ground level. Indeed the area can be thought of as an extension of the New Forest since stock from The Forest was impounded at the cottage known as Poundside after it had wandered in a northerly direction. Today the link still remains through the Earldoms woodlands leading into Langley Wood, which was designated a National Nature Reserve in the mid 1990s. More recently these woods have been included in the New Forest Heritage Area.

Two major changes in woodland management have taken place over the past fifty years or so. Firstly grazing has ceased with the result that the shrubs, saplings and ground flowering plants have increased. The second change, which has occurred in some parts not included within the SSSI, is that from mixed broadleaved species to conifers. One of the aims of the government agency, The Forestry Commission, which was established in 1919, was to increase the production of home grown timber and reduce Britain's dependency on imports. Areas such as Barnsell and Peaks Copse were planted during the period 1945 - 70 and some of the timber is reaching maturity at this time. Unfortunately, our need for timber has escalated such that our UK products remain of little significance and The Forestry Commission now recognises the importance of our woodlands not only as sources of timber but also as wildlife refuges and as areas for recreation. In providing grants for woodland owners consideration is given to all of these aspects and the aim, where practicable, is to produce multifunctional woods.

Wild Service-tree   Sessile Oak   Pedunculate Oak   Small-leaved Lime

Fortunately in Whiteparish the clear-felling prior to replanting with conifers was incomplete and several old trees of a particularly interesting species, sessile oak, remain today, together with some hybrids with its close relative pedunculate oak. The sessile oak is rare in Wiltshire and in The Wiltshire Flora (Gillam 1993) it was recorded in only 1% of the 3792 1 kilometre squares into which the county was divided for recording purposes. The tree is much more typical of the New Forest because it is associated with well drained acidic soils. As well as several specimens in Barnsell and Peaks Copses, they also grow along the parish boundary banks adjacent to the roadside and close to the lay-by formed from the disused section of the old A36. In the same area two other very unusual trees can be found, wild service tree and small-leaved lime. The former is present as young saplings, as regenerating coppice stools and as mature trees. (Coppicing is the practice of growing multi-stemmed trees and shrubs for seven to ten years, then cutting them back to ground level and allowing them to sprout again.) Wild service trees are rarely found in any number and the evidence of regeneration from seed at Whiteparish is encouraging and interesting. Mature specimens have been located also in Bushy Copse and in an unnamed copse opposite Dairyhouse Farm. Small-leafed lime is regarded by some authorities (Rackham 1986) as "a living link with Mesolithic times". (The Mesolithic period extends between 10 000 and 4500 BC and analysis of pollen indicates that lime was the commonest tree in the woodlands of lowland England at that time.) Mature trees grow in Barnsell and Banks Copses and in Whiteparish and Holmere Commons. Particularly fine lines of trees extend along banks, including the parish boundary bank, to both the west and east of the lay-by previously mentioned.

All of the three species named above are native to Britain and are indicative of a long period of woodland cover. Since all are rare, to find the three in one location is regarded as most significant (Colbourn 1983). The boundary banks on which some of the specimens are growing also merit attention. Rackham (1986) states that "Many a parish boundary on the modern map exactly corresponds to an Anglo-Saxon perambulation, which in turn may be interpreted as the boundary of a Roman or Iron-Age estate. Until the early Norman period, minor changes were possible in order to keep lands in one ownership within the same administration. In about 1180 the system froze and could no longer be altered when land changed hands". Therefore it is possible that the woodbanks around the Earldoms area are of the order of eight centuries old. Christopher Taylor, an author of many publications concerning landscape history, and a resident of the parish during the 1960s, states " The whole of Whiteparish Common and the surrounding area is immensely important in terms of the understanding of the English Landscape and especially that part of it concerned with the exploitation of woodland in the past. The area has become well-known in academic circles as a form of type-site for landscape history". (Pers.comm. 1993)

Thus it can be seen that Whiteparish Common is of considerable interest, and not only to those who live locally. Apart from its historical interest it has been noted by natural historians, and in particular by butterfly enthusiasts, in the recent past. Butterfly records from the 1950s are impressive although sadly today many of the species are extinct from the area. In The Butterflies of Wiltshire (Fuller 1995) many references to the species present both at this time and today can be found. It is probable that the more open nature of the woodland during the middle of the century, caused both by grazing and timber felling, provided a warmer, sunnier habitat for these insects. Some of the larger woodland butterflies such as the silver-washed fritillary, white admiral and purple emperor are still to be found in high summer. Others, like the pearl-bordered fritillary and wood white have declined not only in these woods but also nationally.

The range of moths recorded from this location is also impressive and well-known moth collectors frequented the area in the past. The records from these times include a host of species, which today are considered to be rare, and some Red Data Book species (a species located in 15 or fewer 10km2 in

UK). Moth traps set during the 1990s have shown that the area still supports a good range of species, which includes some of the rarities previously identified.

The shaded conditions, moisture-retaining soils and long period of woodland history provide excellent conditions for fungi, ferns and some flowering plants. Seventy-two species of fungi were recorded by Salisbury Natural History Society in 1967 and, of these, four were classed as uncommon and one as rare. The fungi are one of few groups whose diversity has probably been increased by the planting of conifers. The ferns include several, such as narrow-leaved buckler and hard fern, which grow only on ancient woodland sites. Indeed the number of plants found which can be regarded as indicators of the longevity of the site is considerable and includes wood anemone, pignut, wood spurge, tutsan, slender St Johns wort, yellow archangel, yellow pimpernel, butchers broom, wood sanicle and early dog violet.

Up until the late 1930s, red squirrels (sometimes referred to as `snuggies` by local people) were abundant in these woodlands. But, as happened in so many other parts of the country, they were gradually displaced by the spread of the more adaptable grey squirrels, and by the early 1950s they had vanished. In a rather similar fashion, fallow deer used to be much the commonest deer in the parish, but roe and muntjac have now largely displaced them. Badgers and foxes are numerous with large setts and earths in many locations on sands and chalk where the soil is not too heavy. Although tuberculosis is found in badgers in the south-west of the country, and it is believed that badgers may be responsible for passing this disease to cattle, there are no known recorded incidents of TB in the local badger populations.

There have also been changes among the woodland birds. One of the older inhabitants of Whiteparish describes the courtship flight and drumming of snipe in spring, which used to be a common occurrence particularly in boggy areas along Parkwater Road. In the same area, water rails used to be seen occasionally and nightjars could be heard at dusk until about ten years ago. It is doubtful whether any of these are still there today. Nightingales also used to breed along this road but they are no longer heard at Cowesfield Green and only rarely along

Common Road, where the blackthorn bushes used to be a favourite haunt. Barn owls have also decreased, but the odd bird can sometimes be seen at Cowesfield Gate. The pond at Cowesfield Lodge, now much reduced in size, used to attract mallard. One very dry summer, when the pond almost dried up, herons were seen descending on the pond in large numbers. They had located eels in the clay forming the bottom of the pond. (R. Elkins, pers. comm. 1999)

Other woodlands and wetlands. In Lowdens Copse at Ashdod Farm a large pond was dug in about 1930 to attract wild duck, mainly mallard, for sporting purposes. Although partially silted up, mallard are still attracted to this pond when the water level is high enough, and are shot during the winter months. In October 1983, 14 mandarin, including 4 adult males, were recorded on the pond. This handsome duck was introduced into Britain in the early part of this century, originally onto ornamental waters. It has now spread, and breeds freely where conditions are suitable, Virginia Water in Surrey being one of its strongholds. Ashdod Pond, with the dense cover provided by overhanging trees, is typical habitat for this duck. Although only once recorded there since 1983, it is regularly seen on a tiny pond in woodland about 600m further south, which also attracts mallard. Another example of an artificial pond is the one known as the long pond on Newhouse Estate which, until the boundary change 20 years ago, was in the parish of Whiteparish. The pond is believed to have been made during the last century, and the woodland setting, together with dense planting of rhododendrons along one side is clear evidence that it was intended primarily to attract

duck. Ornamental plants were also introduced into the pond and some of these have increased to the extent that there is now a large and spectacular population of greater spearwort, together with yellow loosestrife and bogbean. A less welcome plant is the small, invasive New Zealand pigmyweed which, in 1996, was found on the muddy bottom when the pond had all but dried up during a hot summer spell. The first Wiltshire record for this plant was in 1979 in the north of the county. By 1991 it had spread to the Salisbury area and to West Wellow (Gillam 1993)

Many of the woods within the parish, particularly those to the north such as Gatmore Copse and Mean Wood, were traditionally managed as coppice with standards. The widely spaced standards, planted amongst the coppice stools, provided long-term timber requirements whilst the understory of hazel was coppiced on a 7-10 year rotation. The products of this were used to make thatching spars and hurdles and the residues were made into faggots and used to fire a local bread oven in the parish. Many of the hurdles were used as temporary sheep enclosures and so copses of this type are often located on or near to the downlands where sheep were farmed. The practice of cutting an area or coupe of hazel within a copse to ground level each year led to the proliferation of ground flora such as bluebells, primroses and wood anemone. Although much of our woodland is  no longer coppiced regularly, these plants are still present in profusion in spring when carpets of bluebells can be found in Mean Wood, around Cowesfield and in many other sites.

Some woodland plants are found more commonly on chalky, alkaline soils whilst others favour the acidic soils. Because both soil types occur within the parish, the flora is correspondingly more diverse. Early purple orchids, butterfly orchids, moschatel and Solomon`s seal can all be found in woodlands on Dean Hill, as can the unusual toothwort, a parasite on the roots of hazel. Butcher`s broom grows in many woodland edges in the north-eastern part of the parish and extends southwards into the New Forest. Heathers, ling and bell heather (both of which are very rare in the county), can be found on the sandy soils towards Landford together with other acid-loving plants such as cow wheat and bilberry.

Chalk grasslands. Turning from the wooded areas of the parish to those, which are actively farmed, it is evident that changes over the last 100 years in agricultural practice have had a profound effect upon the wildlife. The ease with which modern ploughs can convert all but the steepest chalk grassland slopes into cultivated, arable land has done much to alter both the frequency and quality of this habitat within the parish. Downland has traditionally been farmed by grazing sheep and, although the slopes on the north side of Dean Hill are still managed in this way, there are very few examples remaining within the parish.

One of the most interesting downland sites is that of Pepperbox Hill, which is included in the Brickworth Down and Dean Hill SSSI. There has been open public access to this site for much of this century and until World War II it was grazed by cattle. It has been owned by the National Trust since the 1930s and is now used by local people, most of whom arrive by car, for walking, kite flying and other recreational pursuits. English Nature (then known as the Nature Conservancy Council) designated it an SSSI in 1951 because of its high quality chalk grassland with nationally restricted plant and butterfly species and because it has one of the largest colonies of regenerating juniper in Hampshire or Wiltshire.

Lack of grazing for some 60 years, other than by rabbits (which were themselves severely reduced in the early 1950s by the disease myxomatosis), has led to the invasion of scrub species such as buckthorn, blackthorn, wild privet, spindle, whitebeam and wayfaring-tree. Indeed, the site can now be regarded as an excellent example of the succession from open grassland to woodland. The management policy of the National Trust is to redress the balance of scrub to open grassland and maintain about 40% scrub and 60% grassland. This is being achieved by scrub clearance of designated areas and is maintained by periodic grazing with New Forest ponies.

Chalk grassland is highly alkaline and nutrient poor, so that vigorous grasses fail to dominate. Such areas are able to support a wide range of plants, which compete with each other so forming a rich mosaic. This flower-rich turf offers both nectar and food plants for numerous insects if grazing by either rabbits or ponies is not too intense during the early summer period. Several species of orchid have been found on the downs, including common spotted, fragrant, pyramidal, bee orchid, burnt orchid, frog orchid, twayblade and autumn lady's tresses. Although prolific in the early 1970s, orchid numbers have declined in recent years and it is hoped that the current management practice will reverse this trend. Other plants found on Pepperbox Hill include bulbous buttercup, small scabious, field fleawort, stemless thistle and dropwort. Most of these plants will only grow in old-established turf, perhaps that which has not been ploughed for as long as one hundred years. Consequently, such plants are rare today and some seed of field fleawort has been collected from this site for the National Millennium Seedbank at Kew Gardens.

The only other traditional downland site of appreciable size within the parish lies along Dean Hill within the Ministry of Defence property (RNAD West Dean). Only a small part of the site lies in Whiteparish but this does include some of the more interesting grassland and scrub. This area was home to a marvellous collection of anthills until the early 1980s when it was disc harrowed, fertilised and reseeded. The work was not very successful and much of the flora has re-established itself, although the same cannot yet be said for the ants.

The areas of downland described above generally abut arable fields where cereal crops are now grown in intensive fashion. The introduction of insecticide seed dressings, chiefly chlorinated hydrocarbons, in the middle of the century led to a marked decrease in raptors all over the country. Curlews were seen on the fields near Pepperbox Hill until 1980s but chemical applications and management changes have brought about their demise. Although many raptors, such as kestrels, sparrow hawks and buzzards declined over the twenty or so years between 1960 -80, they have now substantially recovered as less toxic, more biodegradable chemicals are used on the farmland.

Arable fields. Modern farming methods have also had an impact on the traditional weeds of arable fields. Many of these plants are annuals that depend upon disturbance created by ploughing for their survival and were common until improvements in seed-cleaning techniques reduced their spread. The use of selective weedkillers also has had a great impact on these once common plants although some can still be found growing in odd corners where chemical sprays have not reached. Particularly interesting is the pheasant's eye which used to grow at the edge of an arable field on Moor Farm, but has not been seen for some years. Corn cockle is another rare plant that used to be a common cornfield weed and these two, together with many others, are causing concern not only because of their own demise but also because of the impact this is having on seed-eating birds. The Royal Society for the Protection of Birds is currently funding research into the status and distribution of many of the more threatened species. As is always the case, nature abhors a vacuum and so other more resistant species such as cleavers and field speedwell are showing a marked increase and occupying the niche left vacant.

One type of land management that has had a profound effect on natural history, and particularly on the flora of the affected area, is the European Community's set-aside policy, whereby an area of farmland is taken out of cultivation and allowed to remain fallow for a period of years or put to approved non-agricultural use. Following this five-year period, the same land may be eligible for the optional habitat scheme for a further twenty years, with the object of benefiting the wildlife of the area. Each scheme is accompanied by financial compensation at a fixed rate per hectare. A good example of these schemes can be seen in the two large fields on the south side of Dean Hill forming part of Dean Hill Farm.

Until 1988 cereal crops were grown in these fields, which in consequence underwent an annual cycle of cultivation, seeding and harvesting. Over that period the usual cornfield flowers and weeds were in evidence, including wild oat, corn marigold, common poppy and the rare rough poppy. All these flourish in soil that is ploughed annually, but soon after the set-aside agreement came into operation they were no longer seen. For a few years the two species of fluellen could be found in relatively bare patches, but very soon these and other annual weeds gave way to a complete ground cover consisting of grasses and a large number of different herbaceous perennials. In addition to the obvious colonisers such as dandelions, thistles and docks, the species list now includes coltsfoot, willowherbs (several), broomrape (two species), ploughman's spikenard, orange hawkweed, bristly oxtongue and blue fleabane, together with a few aliens such as Canadian goldenrod, Michaelmas daisy and pearly everlasting. During the last few years there has been a massive increase in beaked hawk`s-beard, so that in May both fields are yellow with this member of the daisy family. In places there has been invasion by scrub, consisting principally of hawthorn, dogwood, whitebeam, hazel, birch, dog rose, brambles and old man`s beard. The seed of these shrubby species has evidently come from the hedge separating the two fields and from a few small copses on the field margins. In the past two years single specimens of broom, buddleja and juniper have also appeared. Despite the reversion to scrub that has occurred over more than a decade, it is interesting to note how quickly some of the former annual plants can return as a result of soil disturbance. During a very wet spell in February 1999 a heavy tractor was driven over one of the set-aside fields leaving ruts at least a foot deep. In June plants of three uncommon annuals - rough poppy, dwarf spurge and Venus's looking glass - were all flowering in one of the ruts. This shows that the seed-bank of some of these annuals is viable over quite a long time span.

Some species of mammal have found the set-aside fields to their liking, including roe deer, badgers, foxes, hares and voles. In fact this is one of the few sites in the parish where hares can be seen regularly. The voles in their turn have attracted raptors - kestrels hunting over the fields are a common sight throughout the year while from November to March hen harriers can occasionally be seen gliding low down over the ground and every now and then pouncing on their unsuspecting prey. In spring, skylarks can be heard singing over the fields and, judging by the numbers seen on the wing during the summer months, there is no dearth of breeding birds. This is against the national trend; skylarks being one of the species that has decreased substantially over much of Britain. In former times, when the fields were ploughed in the autumn, there was always a mass of gulls, rooks and pigeons eating grubs that came to the surface in the newly turned soil. Their place has now been taken by flocks of goldfinches feeding on the thistle seeds.

During the transition from arable to set-aside, some strange plants can be found, often for only a year or two, in conditions far removed from their normal habitat. On Tower Farm, just to the south of Dean Hill Farm, trailing St John`s wort suddenly appeared in some numbers the year after the set-aside agreement was reached. This plant is normally found on acid soils, whereas the field in question is on chalk, so it is a mystery how it got there and why it appeared to be doing so well for that one year. Its rapid demise was probably due to competition from grasses and other much stronger growing perennials. Two other species that appeared briefly on this same farm in 1989 were lesser snapdragon, which is more often a garden weed, and yellow bristle-grass, which is said to be common in birdseed mixtures. Further north, on the very top of Dean Hill, the changed habitat proved just right for Canadian fleabane and prickly lettuce, which appeared in abundance in 1991. Both are conspicuous members of the daisy family, standing 21/2-3 ft tall, so are not easily missed. After two years the numbers rapidly diminished and they have not been seen since. According to the Wiltshire Flora both species were introduced into Wiltshire during the present century, and have spread rapidly in recent years. Other species that, by contrast, appear to have taken up permanent residence in the same field include restharrow, wild mignonette and wild parsnip, along with a host of other common perennials.

Permanent pastures are a feature of the heavier clay soils in the centre of the parish and they extend also to the south where they are frequently interspersed amongst the woodlands. Some are managed as part of a farming system while others comprise one or two fields attached to a private dwelling and may be used for pony grazing. Although difficult to document, it is these areas which have most probably undergone significant changes during the century. The threats are diverse and include not only sale of land for building of new houses but also changes of management such as drainage, ploughing, fertilising or even abandonment.

One field on heavy clay, and with a gentle slope which deterred the use of machinery, supported colonies of common spotted and the more rare green-winged orchids until about 1990. Wood anemone, bugle, sneezewort, meadow sweet and dyer`s greenweed can also be found here but management changes, from late summer grazing - after a hay crop had been taken from the flatter parts of the field - to putting cattle on in early May, has reduced diversity.

Common spotted orchids can be found in many parts of the parish since they seem to flourish on downlands, pasture and woodland. At times they have been prolific along verges of the A36 particularly around the Pepperbox Hill area and at Earldoms. Numbers appear to build up after disturbance, when there is little competition from other vegetation and they decline as coarse grasses and scrub develops. Southern marsh orchids are more rare and are confined mainly to the wetter, acidic fields in the south around the Parkwater area. On occasions they hybridise with the common spotted orchid to produce particularly large plants with conspicuous black rings on the leaves. These have been found on the extreme southwest of the parish along a public right of way leading west from the A36 near Chadwell Farm.

Some of the poorly drained fields around Parkwater and Cowesfield are very rich in plant species. These include not only the orchids mentioned above but also species such as water avens, lesser spearwort, water dropwort, marsh and fen bedstraws, marsh fleawort, marsh woundwort and the two species of skullcap. In these fields also it is not unusual to come across a basking grass snake whilst adders are known to frequent the adjacent woodlands.

A particularly species-rich group of fields lay to the west of the A36 at Chadwell. Until well into the 1990s these fields were managed in a traditional manner by being cut for hay fairly late in the season. Unfortunately, farmers with a small acreage and limited machinery have found it hard in recent times to find contractors to cut their hay and so the fields fall into neglect. For a few years this might seem beneficial to the plants growing there but before long competition becomes rife and diversity decreases. Inevitably the next stage involves sale of land, new ownership and new management. Sometimes conservation bodies such as The Wiltshire Wildlife Trust are able to purchase these meadows or to liaise with the owners concerning their management. However this prospect can, to some owners, seen frightening and the suggestion of a designation such as SSSI status is restrictive. Sadly, one answer to this dilemma is to destroy the conservation interest - easily achieved with modern machinery and chemicals. Changes such as these are probably one of the greatest threats to small areas of exceedingly rich and interesting flora and fauna.

Around the village itself development has inevitably reduced relic features such as old hedges and large orchards, both of which lend a rural feel to the community. Several tracks and lanes lead from the village and these can be havens for wildlife. One of the oldest, if disturbed, pieces of grassland in any village is the churchyard. The significance of `God`s Acre` has been recognised over the past twenty years and books have been written on the subject. Some seventy-six species were recorded in All Saints` churchyard in the mid 1980s, none rare or of particular significance, but together making an interesting assemblage of typical grassland plants. Many factors can influence this community: disturbance, introductions onto graves, bringing in gravel for paths and, last but by no means least, the mowing programme. Two plants, which have appeared in recent years, both along the edges of paths, are whitlowgrass and sand spurrey.

Many of the hedges both within and around the village have probably been derived from relics of woodland, which were saved when cutting out woodland developed the field system. Suitable hedge species may well have been selected and others have seeded in as time went by. Working on this principle, Pollard (1974) has concluded that the age of a hedge can be calculated from the number of species occurring within a thirty-yard stretch.

Age of hedge = [110 x number of species] + 30 years

Using this formula, it is possible to suggest that the hedge bordering the track from Cottage Farm, Common Road, leading into the fields is many hundred years old and the same is undoubtedly true of many other hedges. A little common sense needs to be applied when using the formula, since it is all too clear that today an `old` hedge could be created from a single visit to a suitable nursery!

One of the more significant changes to our hedges has been the demise of the English elm. These trees grew both as suckers in the hedges and as standard trees along Common Road and in many other places; two particularly splendid trees grew near to Courtens Garden Centre at Cowesfield. During the 1970s an outbreak of Dutch elm disease brought about the death of most of these trees although their suckers survived and grew. Unfortunately, as they begin to mature and form young trees after about twenty years, they become susceptible to the fungus and die.

Associated with large beech trees, such as those that grow along Dean Hill, is a quite different fungus, the much sought after truffle. Lillian Moody, who lived in the village for many years, was the granddaughter of Eli Collins of Winterslow, a man well known for his ability to hunt truffles. Mrs Moody wrote an account of her family's long-standing tradition in the `Countryman` (Spring 1979) and mentions near-by Longford Park as an important hunting ground. Stories of them being found within the parish are therefore quite feasible.

Interesting plants have been found in hedges in the village, most notably The Duke of Argyll's Tea Plant, a species introduced from China and grown as hedging but in this village, now removed. Although the reason for the naming of Hop Gardens is not clear, it is interesting to note that hops feature in the hedges in the lane. The plant is native but is often an escape, so offering little help in the understanding of the derivation of the name. Several orchards and hedges along Common Road provide a mass of snowdrops each winter but again, such plants were probably introduced since there are few, if any, records of snowdrops in the south of the county which cannot be associated with old habitations. Other plants, which can be found growing in hedges and on walls in the village, include greater celandine, pellitory of the wall, green alkanet and even cyclamen, which have escaped from gardens. The relatively natural hedges and lanes have provided habitats for many butterflies. The native species such as peacock, small tortoiseshell, brimstone and comma are occasionally joined by immigrants such as the Painted Lady and Clouded Yellow. In 1996 vast migrations of Painted Lady reached Britain from their breeding grounds around the desert edges of North Africa and Arabia. Unfortunately, the butterfly has no hibernating stage in its life cycle and the caterpillar cannot withstand temperatures below 5oC. They therefore perish each winter and new immigrants must find our shores every year. Numbers have now reverted to the usual few seen each summer, in contrast to 1996 when they were more frequent than our common native species.

Collared doves took up residence around the village in 1960s, having been first recorded in Britain in 1955. Numbers have since fluctuated, but they are still fairly abundant. In contrast, turtledoves have decreased sharply over much of Britain although they can still be seen and heard in Whiteparish. Some large rookeries have been fragmented in recent times because their favoured trees have been felled or have died. Two common garden birds, house sparrows and song thrushes, have both shown national and local reductions in number. In the latter instance this has been attributed to the use of slug pellets to kill snails, although another possible explanation could be the increase in sparrow hawks in recent years. Another possible culprit could be the magpie, which has also increased as game keeping and shooting have declined.

Ponds in the vicinity of the village - at the recreation ground, off Dean Lane (near Alderstone House) and along Common Road (opposite Bartes Farm) - are becoming enclosed by trees and are in danger of silting up. Newts have been found at the first of these and some 25 or more years ago there were so many frogs mating at the Common Road pond that the bus stopped to allow people to view! Garden ponds, which are so much better maintained, are undoubtedly more significant in the lives of these creatures today. Frog populations are, however, declining at this time due to disease and possibly to environmental changes.

We hope that this short article will give readers some idea of the natural history of our parish at the end of the millennium and the changes, as we see them, which have occurred in the recent past. We have made no attempt to list, or even include, all of the plants and animals which frequent our parish but some of this information can be found in books which have been published over the years. Detailed records are kept also at the Biological Records Centre in Devizes. The following is a list of useful sources of information and includes the references cited in the text.

Jeremy Wood
Pat Woodruffe
June 1999

Colbourn P. 1983 Hampshire's Countryside Heritage - Ancient Woodland. Hampshire County Council, Winchester.

Collins L. 1979 England's Last Truffle Hunters. The Countryman, Burford.

Fuller M. 1995 The Butterflies of Wiltshire. Pisces Publications, Newbury.

Gillam B. 1993 The Wiltshire Flora. Pisces Publications, Newbury.

Greenoak F. 1985 God's Acre. Orbis.

Grose D. 1957 The Flora of Wiltshire. Wiltshire Archaeological & Natural History Society, Devizes.

Pollard E, Hooper M.D. and Moore N.W. 1974 Hedges The New Naturalist, Collins.

Rackham O. 1986 The History of the Countryside. Dent.

Recording Wiltshire's Biodiversity. Wiltshire and Swindon Biological Records Centre, Wiltshire Natural History Forum, Devizes.

Salisbury Natural History Society Records

Stearn L.F. 1975 Supplement to the Flora of Wiltshire. Wiltshire Archaeological & Natural History Society, Devizes.

Taylor C.C. 1967 Whiteparish - A study of the development of a forest-edge parish. Wiltshire Archaeological & Natural History Magazine No. 62 pp79-102. Devizes.

Wiltshire Biological Records Centre, Devizes.

Wiltshire Botany. Journal of the Wiltshire Botanical Society, Devizes.

Wiltshire Wildlife Trust. Devizes.

CHAPTER 3

THE PARISH COUNCIL

The following is the order of events within the parish as gleaned from the minutes of the Parish Council through the 100 years. The early minute books, which are kept in the County Archives at Trowbridge, are fine books, well bound and the copper plate writing of the secretary of the day is a work of art. We do in fact go back six years, prior to the beginning of the century to 1894 which is worth doing because that is the start of the era of local democracy in the country. It was on a Tuesday in December a meeting was called in the schoolroom to elect the first Council. Eighty-three people were present; it must have been a crush! Squire Lawrence proposed that Lord Nelson should chair the meeting, this proposal was carried. The reason for this meeting was to select candidates for the election of parish councillors.

Lord Nelson proposed an informal rule that during the evening there was to be no barracking by those present, no speeches made and a show of hands would be the voting procedure. Nineteen names were put forward as candidates. A fortnight later, on December 15th 1894 a poll was held, using ballot papers and the following were elected: -

Squire Lawrence	111 votes
Dr Key-Wells, Medical Practitioner	87 votes
Mr J Clayman, farmer	87 votes
Mr Champion, farm bailiff	85 votes
Mr E Elkins, dealer	81 votes
Mr I Giles, gardener	78 votes
Mr J Drake, woodsman	77 votes
Mr Fulford	75 votes
Mr J Betteridge, farmer	71 votes
Mr Snelgrove, farmer	71 votes
Mr Lampard, carrier	67 votes

There were 168 papers recorded, three spoilt papers, thirteen illiterates and one blind voter. 202 voters were registered in the parish and it is interesting to note the landlord/farmer dominance, indicating the dependence on farming to the village.

The very first meeting was held on December 31st 1894 at 7 pm in the rectory room. The first chairman was Squire Lawrence MP, Mr Williams was clerk, at that time called an Overseer, he had an assistant Mr Page who actually took over in January on the death of Mr Williams. The Election cost £6. The first precept was £30 (according to the Oxford Dictionary a precept is 'an order for collection or payment of money under a rate.)

At this stage the Rev. Patterson handed over the administration of the Village Charities to the Council also three large books (from whom it is not recorded) the Poor book, 1788 - 1817, Charity accounts 1841 - 1872 and school accounts 1859 - 1874.

An early photo of 'the Lynches'

At the annual meeting in the reading rooms (The Lynches) a technical committee was formed to investigate the work of the college for women formed at Trowbridge. It was connected with the Wiltshire School of Cookery. Ten lessons on Cookery could be had for five shillings. Grants could be obtained for up to £1 10/-. Home nursing lessons cost 1/- per head. The cooking lessons gave instructions in baking bread, pastry, steak pie, Christmas pudding, soups, cakes and cottage pie.

From this point we report only the main events which come to light from the minutes, the dates being given.

1901

At the annual parish meeting, water came under discussion. People in Common Road who paid rent to Lord Nelson had to go some 400 yards for drinking water. The Council wrote to his Lordship asking if he would put in a supply. His reply was to the effect that if the Council wanted to do the job he had no objections! The charges for the use of wells were then recorded. Swan cottage on the Street charged 1/6d per household. The owner of Well House charged 1/6d for a key to the well door and the Fountain charged 6d per person. In some cases a rope and bucket was included and in others folk had to bring their own.

1905

A motorist was reported speeding through the village and the County Council was asked to erect a sign as the bends and undulations in the road made walking dangerous. A committee was appointed to measure the road width in the Street and count the number of houses.

Newton Corner, the crossroads mentioned in the text.

1907

More complaints on speeding. A horse killed by a car at the Newton Lane corner. Allotment and Smallholders Act was brought in and required the Council to list the smallholdings under 50 acres in the parish. There were 35 smallholdings. Villagers could apply to the Parish Council for an allotment of up to five acres or even a smallholding of up to 50 acres, the County Council would buy the land. Only one man applied.

1910

A second Post delivery came into being, an additional delivery being made at mid-day.

1914

The Council was involved in a dispute with Lord Nelson about the overgrown common. Commoners said the grazing was being reduced. No satisfactory reply came from Lord Nelson so the dispute was sent to the Courts Baron, who apparently ruled then on Common land problems. A Mr Cook who lived at Cowesfield had died of TB. A row developed because the Sanitary Inspector had not disinfected the house for over two months. Residents in the Hop Gardens wanted the road adopted, Parish Council was asked to support. Precept £5. Clerk asked for an increase of salary to £5 pa, due to war inflation.

1917

Request for Wiltshire County Council to Tar the Street, turned down.

1918

War Agricultural Committee demand cultivation of neglected allotments. No workers could be found to do the work. At the annual meeting of 1918 angry farmers wanted to know why the deer park owned by Miss Bristowe (at Broxmore) was not ploughed up, when they had orders to plough land that was almost impossible to get a plough into.

1919

The Council was informed that War Trophies could be obtained from some army barracks and it was suggested that small trophies could be given to village institutions. On offer were anti-tank guns, rifles, cartridge boxes, body armour, helmets, and wire cutters. A Councillor went to see what was available at Devizes, came away with only three old rifles at a cost of 13/2^1/2d. These were given to the school.

1921

Mr Spark offered to buy land on which to build a village hall, site almost as now. The offer was accepted. An ex-army hut in sections, which was proposed to be used as a hall, was already in Parsonage meadow. A big debate took place before the Council accepted the offer of the present site. The Council was asked for information on village housing needs. Estimated population 992, houses 208. Eight new houses were asked for but at a cheap rent. Precept £5.

1924

The Council was requested to stop charabanc passengers from singing and cheering when coming through the village street at night! A 10 miles an hour speed limit was asked for.

1929

A letter was sent to Lord and Lady Melchet thanking them for money given by them towards the cost of the new village hall.

THE WATER SUPPLY at Whiteparish, Wilts. Owing to the drought water has to be

'Villagers collecting water during drought 1930s'

Water being distributed in December 1933

1934

There were extraordinary problems of water supply in the village. At an open meeting called in July it was reported that Squire Lawrence's supply from Gatmore was not capable of meeting all needs. Help from the County Council was sought when it was suggested that a loan could be obtained for a new supply. The first of many discussions were started about a new recreation ground. It was suggested that Parsonage meadow was a possibility. Precept £20, clerk's wages remained unchanged at £5 pa.

1935

Squire Lawrence MP JP died. He had not only owned 1400 acres of the land in the parish but also had the Church, the school and Parish Council at heart. Many people attended his funeral from far and wide. After his death, Chairmen of the Council started to come from men in more varied walks of life. At a meeting called in May help was sought for those who had lost all in the fire of several cottages in Bunkers Hill. Sherfield English sent £12 towards the fund. A great deal of pressure was coming from parishioners regarding lack of an electricity supply, it was said that "villages and hamlets all round have it why not Whiteparish?" Post Office to close for half day on Thursdays, there were no objections. The Lynches was sold by the Coles family and a comment was made that "all that had met there for years chucked out without a by your leave". The Parish Council offered to rent rooms for the Youth Club, a Reading room and a place for the Council to meet.

1936

A bus shelter was erected with £10 offered by Wiltshire and Dorset Bus Company towards the cost. An accident occurred at Newton Lane crossroads, there were two cars involved. Precept £40, clerks salary £20 pa.

1938 - There were still demands for electricity and water supplies to be installed.

1939 - 1945

Because of the war the Parish Council kept its activities to a minimum, but each year the annual Parish meeting was held and charity work continued.

1946-1964

Until 1964 the work of the Council was almost mundane dealing with footpath problems, speeding traffic and poor roads. As written elsewhere the Memorial Ground came into being. Water, electricity, sewerage and street lighting were installed. The District Council gave outline planning permission for the Triangle although it was objected to by the Parish Council. A one-way traffic system around the Triangle was suggested.

1966

During this year there was the first indication of the A36 becoming a trunk road. Precept £360.

1968

The Commons Registration Act came into being and the Parish Council had the task of registering the village commons or losing them. The first indication of housing being developed on Chalk Pit Farm.

1970

Meadow Court was named officially. The Clerk's salary was £52. The precept was £225. The proposed development of Sansom's and Young's Farms was first mentioned, 301 houses were proposed. A feeling of a 'cold war' was felt in the village and a need for someone to organise a defence was required but there were no takers. The first indications of Dutch Elm disease were reported.

1972

Dutch Elm disease appears in village trees. The bus service was withdrawn on Sundays, the reason given 'lack of passengers'.

1973 - The first Whiteparish week was celebrated. Precept now £450.

A typical float in the 1991 Whiteparish Week Carnival

1974

Broxmore House development was started. Farmers were enlisted to carry out snow clearance with tractors mounted with snowploughs.

1975

The need for a new Village hall and combined pavilion was first mooted. The police were called out on one occasion to a late night disturbance in the village centre. There were delays in getting plans passed for the new hall and the whole idea was abandoned in 1979.

1976

The parish council asked for gas to be supplied to the village. £80 given towards a Foot Clinic.

1977 - The village hall was valued at £25,000 (for insurance purposes).

1979

The 100 plus Club was started to raise funds to keep the hall in good repair. A Lottery was proposed to raise funds for Youth activities. There was popular demand for more affordable houses for young people. A kitchen extension was built on the village hall. There were problems of encroachment on Common Land. There were first indications of the building of a new Surgery in the village. At a special meeting villagers were able to vote on the proposal, which was carried by a large majority on the 6th September 1979 after much hard debating.

1980 - Precept £1700 and the clerk's salary now stood at £444.

1982

An air survey was made of the whole parish which should be in the Public Records Office at Trowbridge.

1983

A new Youth Club was built by volunteers. Floodlighting of the Church was undertaken and the Parish Council was to pay £394 towards the cost.

1984 - Precept £2,234.

1985

There was an explosion in Paynes Fireworks Factory in the Chalk Pit and there was much concern about village safety. By sheer coincidence the Wiltshire County Council had been asking that a site be made available for a Hydrogen Bomb Shelter.

1987

There was a fatal accident at Brickworth Corner and a letter was sent notifying our local MP Possibility of setting up Neighbourhood Watch schemes was being investigated. A proposal to have cheaper housing through a Housing Association was discussed. Gas mains were laid within the village.

1988

New housing development in Dean Lane is to be named Nunns Court. The Parish Council signed away any responsibility for the Village Hall to the Hall Committee, who will create a Charity. Precept £2750. Secretary's salary £420. Shots were fired in a footpath confrontation.

1989

It was reported to the Parish Council that grass cutting of the Memorial Ground cost £474. The first houses in the Dean Lane and Bramley housing developments were sold. The first Neighbourhood Watch was formed. It was reported that the water supply to the village being in such poor shape a new water main is to be laid.

1990

Once again a proposal for a new village hall was put forward. Precept £2901. It was announced that Whiteparish is now included in the New Forest Heritage boundary.

1992

The village policeman retires and the police house in the village is up for sale, with policing to come from Alderbury. Negotiations are taking place with a Housing Association and that association is prepared to pay £24000 per acre for suitable land, but there were no takers from landowners. The new hospital in Salisbury is to have a ward named Whiteparish.

1993

A waste tip at Whelpley farm was proposed, there were extremely strong objections to the proposal. 37 motorists were caught speeding through the village. Work was started on traffic lights at Brickworth corner. Precept £3000.

1994

Problem have arisen with proposals for the new village hall. The Council is advised that a new burial ground will be needed in 10 years time, and is asked to look for suitable ground, with a compulsory purchase order possible. Precept £5000.

1996

A 'Link' scheme is started with Landford which involves voluntary help for those in need of transport, or other assistance. A telecommunications tower has been built at Earldoms.

1997

Views were taken on what to do for the Millennium celebrations. The Sports Council refuses a grant towards a new village hall. Precept £8000, clerk's salary £1300. There is a noted increase of vandalism in the village.

1998

Once again the Village hall proposal fails to get any grants towards the cost of new building. It was reported that £450,000 would be needed for the entire complex. The Council was notified that there was a Ragwort weed problem along edges of the roads. A camera was bought by Parish Council to record any building activities in the Parish to monitor any planned activities.

1999 - A poll took place to elect Parish Councillors.

The Parish Council 1999, members left to right, back row, Paula Horton, Roly Chalk, Trevor King, Roy Billet, Lorraine Morrish, John Lequesne, Front Row, Colin Bray, Malcolm Simmons, Peter Green and Ann Galvin.

CHAPTER 4

MEMORIES OF OLDER FOLK COLLECTED OVER TWO YEARS.

The late Len Cobern 1911 to 1999

Len Cobern was one of 5 boys all of whom lived to a good age in the village of Whiteparish; in fact Len has lived in his house in Clay Street for 72 years. All the boys attended the village school under the headmaster Mr. Faulkner, who was greatly admired by Len who eventually won a scholarship to Bishop Wordsworth School in Salisbury, which at that time was co-ed. Attending a school in Salisbury at that time involved being a boarder with someone in Salisbury until he was old enough to cycle to school.

Len Cobern's father was born in Broxmore House and worked as a dairyman and gardener all his life. He also used to drive the village doctor in his horse drawn trap when he was visiting patients. He was a keen gardener and kept his family well supplied with produce from the garden but would never allow his sons to help him, although they were allowed to do major work like tree felling or heavy pruning. His employer was Mr Davies of Ashmore House, who would allow Len Cobern's father to use his horse trap to give the boys rides out into other villages, which was a great treat. The father was a fair man who was able to discipline his boys without resorting to the cane or even raising his hand. Len's mother was a member of an old village family, the Chants, and she and her husband would take the boys for walks on fine Sunday evenings which generally meant visiting the New Inn (now The Parish Lantern) with father having his pint and the children having lemonade and crisps. There was no mention of what his mother had to drink. One memorable evening she found a sovereign that was never spent and is still in the family. Mr Cobern senior used to boost his income by cutting the hair of village members for 3d a cut. The boys used to hold a candle so that father could work in the shed in the garden. He also used to mend the family shoes, a common practice in the village.

The Cobern boys did not receive pocket money but earned a few coppers by running errands for others. Old Mrs Woodford, known as 'granny' Woodford would reward him with a 'penny high cake' which was a sort of dough cake. Another treat for all the village children was the wagon rides to Nomansland arranged by the Church and Chapel. Len Cobern remembers on one of these outings sweets being thrown amongst the trees in the forest and the children having to find them, there were no wrappings on the sweets, either!

The family would on occasions walk to West Dean station and catch the train to Salisbury and in the evening take the train back again to West Dean and walk home again, just for the ride on a train. Mr Cobern remembered when he first saw a train arriving at a platform, thinking to himself that the driver must be very clever to bring the train to a stop so near to the platform's edge, he had not realised that the train was on rails.

After the harvest had been gathered, the children of the village were allowed to take little handcarts into the field to glean any wheat left lying in the field. This was taken home, the heads removed from the straw, sacked up and taken to a farm for threshing. The grain was then taken to a mill in Dunbridge to be ground into flour for bread making. The bread made at his home was then taken to an aunt's house for baking as she had a large oven in her house. Later bread was brought round in a cart by one of the many bakers in the village.

Mr Cobern recalled how the headmaster of the school, Mr Faulkner, would collect water from 'the trunk', the well in Hop Gardens near to Samson's Farm, and carry the two bucketsful back to the school. He also remembers that Mrs Faulkner used to put drinking water on the wall between the school and the house next door for the children who were staying at school midday and were having sandwiches for lunch, there were no school dinners in those days. The older boys were taught gardening by Mr Faulkner whilst the girls learned 'housecrafts', the gardeners were allowed to take home the produce of their labours. Mr Faulkner was a very patriotic Briton and would fly a flag from a pole in the school grounds on 'Empire Day', King and Queen's birthdays and other days of national celebration. He was also a keen cricketer and he, and Len Cobern's father would regularly walk from the village to West Tytherly for a cricket match.

Café on Pepperbox Hill

Mr Cobern could just remember the celebrations following the end of World War 1. There was a day of fun and games held on Parsonage Field, which was the village recreation ground. This was on the south side of Common road behind where the row of bungalows is now standing. There was throwing the cricket ball for the women and riding bicycles between obstacles for the children. Also the vicar gave children rides in his car, the only trouble being that so many children enthusiastically climbed into the car that it would not move. All the families went to the fun and games and chatted to each other, as everyone knew everyone else.

In his teenage years Len used to gather with others at Pepperbox hill, where there used to be a little café. This was closed down after it had been broken into and damaged several times. There was a boys club held in the Lynches and on one occasion he remembers a Parish Council Meeting being held on the second floor and the Councillors leaving their hats and coats on the ground floor. One of the boys decided it would be fun to smear the insides of the hats with soot, none of the boys had the nerve to wait to see the results. As the boys grew older they would visit the 'Kings Head' in the evenings.

Pepperbox Hill, the old road running down to Salisbury, showing the café on the brow of the hill

The modern A 36, showing the road from the top of Pepperbox Hill running towards Southampton

Sunday mornings was the time for cleaning and repairing bicycles ready for the coming week of work or school. Employment in the village was predominantly working on farms caring for horses etc. There were three blacksmiths in the village and many small shops. The 'Smithy' behind the Fountain Inn was a wheelwright as well. Mr Cobern and his brothers worked a smallholding for many years but in 1952 they had a serious fire which damaged all the buildings. There was no piped water in the village so the smallholding was ruined. The main supply was 'the Trunk' near Sampson's farm where villagers collected water, always making sure to replace the cover on the well, to keep the water clean.

Mr Cobern remembered the jubilation when water was brought into the village after World War 2. Electricity was in the village just before W W 2.

Mr Cobern could recall when the Chalk Pit, now occupied by Pain's Fireworks, was used to supply local farms with lime for the land. They would bring horse drawn carts and since the sides of the pit were so steep the horses could only pull half loads out, so the men would unload the first half load, go back for a further half load. Having climbed out of the Chalk Pit, they would then have to add the half load already brought out before they could drive back to their farm. The men in the chalk pit would work in harnesses chipping the chalk from the steep face letting the lumps fall to the ground where the waiting farmers could collect it. He could also recall the flint pits near Fuller's Hill, on the north side of the A 27 near Whelpley Farm, being used to supply flints, he assumed, for the roads.

Mrs Hankey of Claremont.

Mrs Hankey's forefathers (possibly paternal great grandfather) came from Scotland in the 1830's. He lived at Earldoms. Her paternal grandfather was born in Earldoms and buried in Whiteparish Churchyard. He owned Little Sutton's on the A 27, which at that time was a grocer's store and bakery. This was for some time before and after 1900. There were three bakeries in the village then. Her father was born in Little Sutton's and died in 1943. He farmed rented land comprising three farms, one called Chalk Pit farm, a dairy farm, where the Pains Fireworks site now is, one at Blaxwell farm and another on the Street called Street farm which was arable. Chalk Pit and Blaxwell farms were rented from Forts of Alderbury and Street farm from the Nelson Estate. There were also many farms in the area rented from the Cowesfield Estate.

Mr Hankey moved to Whiteparish when he and Mrs Hankey married. Mr Hankey was a painter and decorator and his father was a farm manager in West Kirby in 1932. Mrs Hankey was for some years a 'live-in' matron in a Salisbury school but later used to travel to Salisbury in a local bus each day. The buses ran every half-hour from 7am till 11pm until the 1960's when the timetable was altered to make it an hourly service.

Mrs Hankey has lived in 'Claremont' all her life. It was built and completed in May 1910, by Mitchell's of Downton. The sand needed for the mortar etc. was dug from the land on which the house is built, the resulting hole being the cellars beneath the house. It is not known where the bricks were obtained from but at the time there were 2 brick kilns in the village, one near the Doctor's surgery and another on the site of Grahams at the end of Common Road.

Mrs Hankey's home 'Claremont'

Mrs Hankey's memories relate, on the whole, to the years between the two World Wars.

Water supply has always been difficult in Whiteparish (until piped in much later). Claremont had its own well as did many other houses in the village, but there were public wells, a well on the site of the village hall (which was then a rifle range) and in the grounds of the Post Office. There was also a good spring called 'the trunk' in Hop Gardens from which the headmaster at the school had to collect water for the school's use. Oil lamps and candles lighted Claremont like many other houses.

Mrs Hankey remembers how the Common which is the land opposite the school, now privately owned, was used to graze cattle, sheep, and also at times geese. There were very few houses in Common Road then, the Bramley's estate was in fact an orchard. Cattle used to be driven to various ponds in the village to be watered and older folk used regularly to glean in harvested fields.

The village population was very reliant on farming and farm labouring, also as staff in the various big houses. Although not a wealthy village the villagers were very generous in supporting money-raising efforts, when such demands were made. There was very little opportunity for most people to get out of the village and to mix with others. The Salisbury fair was a great attraction, and Sunday school outings, usually on a horse drawn wagon to Nomansland, were a great treat to children. There is a story of an old villager, who had never left the village in his life, being taken to Downton to view the trains and being surprised by the fact that there were two trains in the station at one time. Marriage between village families was very common.

In the very early days Mr Bailey ran a horse and chaise to carry people into town. Later Mr Lampard and then Mr Kemish ran a pony and trap service to Salisbury on Tuesdays and Saturdays (market days to this day) and to Southampton on Mondays and Thursdays. The fares were 1/3d to Salisbury return and 1/9d to Southampton return. The Wilts and Dorset Bus Co. bought out Mr Bailey.

There were very few telephones in the village, but there was one in the Post Office and later in the Butcher's shop.

There was a path called Cinder path which ran from Miles Lane (then called 40 Acre Lane) to the Romsey Road which was surfaced with cinders from the boilers of the Greenhouses at Cowesfield house so as to make the walk to church a dryer and more comfortable walk for the staff of that house. Today it is still a bridle path.

During World War 11 the forces requisitioned the large houses in the area. Cowesfield housed the Americans, Broxmore the Poles.

Mrs Hankey's father Mr Page was clerk to the Parish Council for more than 40 years. She remembers the minutes of the meetings being written up by her father in a large suede covered book. The Parish Council meetings were held in an upstairs room in the Lynches, which for many years before had been the village, work house and later became the village reading room and also a place for younger members of the village to gather to talk and play billiards.

Mr Page also acted as rate collector, travelling by pony and trap as far afield as Broxmore, Ash Hill, New House and Gatmore; he would often take his daughter with him. She remembers a heavy stick with a metal end, which he used to knock on doors, so loudly that it could not be ignored.

Mr Page also dealt with various trusts that were set up in the village. One was to supply sheets at Christmas time to needy families; these were collected from a warehouse in Salisbury, in pairs, which had to be separated as only one sheet was allowed per family. There was also a fund to allow so many men and so many women to draw an amount of money annually or quarterly. Medical needs were met from yet another fund. There were tithes to be collected from many properties, Rabbit Cottage and Dean Hill Farm being remembered.

There was also a field in Blaxwell Farm called Fisherton which had at sometime a charge (tithe) which went to support almshouses in Fisherton Street in Salisbury. The Hayter Charity supported these houses. The Tithe Barn was on land near the new surgery, there was a pond there too.

Mrs Marjorie Hayes of 'Wickets'

Mrs Hayes remembers the Primitive Methodists Meeting House in Clay Street, a Plymouth Brethren Meeting House next to the School, and a 'Four Gospels' Meeting House in the cottage next to the Fountain Inn as well as the Village Methodists Chapel in Dean Lane. The Village Methodists used to give the children a Christmas party with a Christmas Tree and a marvellous tea. She remembers Sir Adrian Boult's daughter Dorothy presenting prizes on one occasion. The Methodists regularly organised a Sunday school Outing in the summer for around 60 children. They would travel in a wagon pulled by a horse to Nomansland, a rope would be thrown up into a tree to act as a swing, games would be played, and the children would each come home with an orange, a great treat. The 'Band of Hope' was popular with young people and the Chapel used to provide lovely teas that young people and young families attended.

Mrs Hayes home 'Wickets'

Mrs Weedon lived in a cottage on Bunkers Hill, she made vanilla ice cream and on high days she would colour the ice cream pink and sell it as strawberry ice cream. The cost was half an old penny, less than a quarter of a new penny. Mrs Hayes family ran the shop in the village at the Salisbury end of the Street. They sold grocery and china among other things. There was also a shop that sold knitting wools and sewing items, and 'Little Suttons' was still a sweet shop. These shops must have got their stock brought in by carriers from Salisbury or Southampton.

Mrs Hayes family obtained water from the well in the grounds of the cottage opposite, it was beautifully clear. Farmers used to go to Park Water to collect water from the stream there. Dean Hill properties were particularly short of water and in fact brought in a water diviner, it is not known if he had any success. There was a pond near the Scout Hut and there was a pond of poor water up Dean Hill. There is of course the Long pond at Cowesfield and another one near there that had water lilies on it.

Mrs Hayes remembers that five Church cottages, having been bought from the Church, were cleared of the tenants so that the new housing in 'The Green' could be built. She feels that they would not have been pulled down in this day and age, but would have been restored.

The Reading Room in the Lynches was well used and cricket was played on 'Parsonage Field'. There was a village band and dances were held regularly. There was a Drama Group and the Chapel used to hold Concerts and Lantern Slide Shows.

Soldiers were stationed at Cowesfield in huts and many used to attend the Methodist Chapel.

Jack Woodford

Jack Woodford was born in 1904. His father was the baker who lived and worked in the Street and worked with his father the Woodford grandfather. The shop and house was originally rented from the Nelson Estate, which owned the greater part of Whiteparish. Miss Bristowe at Broxmore House also owned a lot of property in the village. Father was a weekend soldier before the Great War and served in the Army in that war. The family all attended the village school, as had Mr Woodford senior. As war work Jack Woodford had to do farm work on a smallholding in Dove's lane working for Mr Collins, from the age of 13, for a wage of 5/- (25p) per week. Mr Collins used to cream off the milk and make butter which was sold around the village, as was the milk for one and a half old pence a pint. In 1918 Jack went to work as a garden boy for 7/- (35p) a week. In 1919 he joined his father (now discharged from the army) looking after the horses that the family owned, as bread was sold round the village from carts drawn by horses. Eventually he learned the baking trade and worked in the bakery for 20 years becoming a master baker.

There were two Baker's rounds; Jacks went out as far as the Hatchet Inn in Sherfield English, including Broxmore House and Cowesfield House.

In 1923 a van was bought to replace the horse drawn carts. Driving the van was a highly skilled occupation as the engine was very primitive, with no synchromesh gears or starter motor. The roads were not made up, just flint surfaces which played havoc with the tyres, an hour or more could pass trying to mend a puncture. At this time water would run down the Street after a rainy period.

The Second World War was declared and in 1940 Jack was called up, at first to act as a driving instructor as not many people could drive in those days. He would train five men at a time, each taking a turn at driving. Later he was on guns defending London during the blitz.

Jack Woodford 'monkeying around' in a village show

He remembers the lawns at the 'big house' (Cowesfield) being cut by a horse drawn mower. The horse had special leather boots to wear to protect the lawns. Cowesfield house owned three horses used for pulling coaches and dog carts. Coaches were used for long journeys and the dogcart for driving into Salisbury, Romsey or Southampton.

As a young boy Jack used to act as beater for various shoots, often their numbers would be increased with soldiers coming in as beaters. He remembers that he did receive payment but he is not sure of the amount. He thinks perhaps 6d (two and a halfpence) and a rabbit to take home, even an occasional pheasant would be hidden away to take home later. They always had a good dinner of soup and stew. Lloyd George was a member of one of the shoots; he was recognised from photographs

Jack was for many years a member of the pantomime cast. Football was another pastime, but that came to an abrupt end when he broke his leg during a game. He ended up in hospital for some time and was unable to work for several weeks. Fortunately the family was insured against injury and they were able to make a claim, as there was no National Health Benefit in those days.

The dances, held in the school, were popular even with the young men. Sometimes a pianist, Mr Lockyer using his own piano, supplied the music, the same piano and pianist entertained at Cricket Club Luncheons. The piano would be carted down to the 'Kings Head' and manhandled up stairs into the Club Room. There used to be a Rifle Club in the village, the practices took place on the site where the village hall now stands. A popular pastime with young men and boys was using catapults to kill squirrels (skuggies) and occasional pheasants, if they had been caught killing pheasants they would have been in real trouble.

There was also a Blacksmith's Shop near where the village hall now stands run by Mr Hinwood. There were three other blacksmiths in the village, one at the back of the Fountain Inn, one near the Lynches and one at Cowesfield Green, the house there is still called 'The Forge'. There was also a local Undertaker - Mr Fred Alford.

Jack Woodford 1999

Vera Fortune and Beth Noyce

Vera Fortune (nee Woodford) was born in 1906 and Beth Noyce (nee Woodford) was born in 1909. Vera remembers going to school in the village in 1910 at the age of 4. The Head Teacher, Mr Faulkner, had asked that she should attend school earlier than usual as the school roll was down at that time

The family had their own house in 'The Street'. The road had grass on each side and became like a stream in wet weather. Mother would collect water from a well ,behind the 'Fountain Inn', that was where there was 'good' water. There were wells in many gardens which was not such good water. Water would be collected every day. Washing was done in 'wash houses' using rainwater. Vera was always afraid of open wells, she knew of one in which a dog had drowned. Father was a local baker and had to

Jack and Vera Woodford around 1910

collect many buckets of water each day for making bread. The schoolmaster fetched water for the school from the 'trunk', a spring in Hop Gardens, carrying the buckets on a yoke.

The remains of the well near Samsons Farm known as the 'trunk', now overgrown but still producing water'

Mother cooked on a kitchen range heated mainly by burning wood, it had a hot water tank on the side. Sundays they would always enjoy a roast dinner, usually beef with yorkshire pudding. Porridge was the usual breakfast, and sometimes as a treat on Saturday mornings they would have egg sandwiches. Mother would buy once washed chitterlings from the butcher for 1/-(5p) and would clean them thoroughly in a big bath. Then the chitterlings were fried. There was also rabbit, pheasant and chicken on the menu.

Both the women remember watching pigs being killed by the local blacksmith and seeing them hung in trees to 'cool'. Eventually the carcass would be taken down, butchered, part smoked and eaten by the owner's family and friends. They feel sure there was no worry of the meat being stolen, the village was a honest place, although they do remember a pig's leg being chewed by a local dog.

Carcass hanging in a tree 'to cool'

They have memories of the Primitive Methodists in Hop Gardens and of a 'meeting house, in the house of their grandmother, next to the 'Fountain Inn' which was used as such only on Sunday mornings. Their father used to make a loaf as their communion bread. They used to attend the 'Band of Hope' which was enjoyed because it was held in the evening, although they were brought up to attend church, they liked the singing. Mr Lockyer looked after the Chapel. They recall the Christmas Tree that was in the Chapel each Christmas as everyone had a present from the tree. The sisters remember the Sunday school outings, their father made the cakes for the children to enjoy.

Mrs Vera Fortune won a scholarship to attend Bishops School in Salisbury when she was 12. She was at first a boarder for a whole term but was very homesick, so her father bought her a bicycle and she would cycle to school on a Monday and home again on Friday evening. They would sometimes get a lift from a carrier who was going into Salisbury. Vera remembers she used to cycle to dances, picking up her long skirts to make the journey possible. Bishops School at that time was a mixed sex school although the girls and boys were taught in separate classes. However social contact was inevitable and Vera has memories of mild flirtations. Both sisters remember the dances held at the village school. Beth was at first too young to go to the dances but remembers attending fancy dress dances. Their mother made all the costumes, on one occasion she was dressed as a Christmas Cracker which was a little too tight round the ankles and split during the parade, also she was once dressed as an Indian prince, even wearing special shoes with turned up toes. Another meeting place for young people was the tea-rooms on Whiteparish Hill (now known as Pepperbox hill)

The Woodford family shop 1902

When Mrs Beth Noyce finished school she went to work in the family shop. Vera at 17 went to help Grandmother in the Post Office until a vacancy came up for a School Mistress. She did not really enjoy teaching but she earned 30/- (£1.50) a week most of which was given to her mother. Mother used half of the money to buy Saving Certificates for Vera's future use.

The Post Office had a switchboard but at first there was only the doctor on the phone, but a man was in the village trying to get others to rent a phone at 2/6d (12 and a half pence) a week. Not many people were prepared to pay that much.

Both the sisters recall the pantomimes put on by the village school. The children were organised by Mrs Harding , the wife of the vicar. Rev. Harding is remembered as a very kindly much loved man. Later as the sisters grew older they were involved with the Drama Club, organised by Miss Stewart who had been an actress. The family was regularly featured in the drama group's presentations throughout the war years and well into the 1950's.

Many men of the village had their social contact in the pubs. The sisters can recall being outside a pub, peeping in the back windows, and their father bringing out a small packet of biscuits for the children. They would often be sent to the pub to remind father that dinner was ready.

When their brother was born mother was told to expect him to die, but was advised to place him in warm water all night and hope that would revive him, which of course it did. The village midwife attended mothers. There was also a woman who was employed to lay out the dead, the doctor would be called only in extreme cases as he had to be paid a fee which many people could not afford. Babies would be fed Nestles Milk if breast milk failed.

Mrs Fortune can remember when she was 16 or 17, villagers were given sheets which were bought with money left in a Trust by a spinster lady, a surviving sister of three. Later the gift was money rather than sheets.

Vera's wedding was a small affair, the family, schoolmaster and teachers attended, there was no honeymoon, generally people went back to work the day following the marriage.

The bells in the church were used to signify a death in the village, it was known by the villagers who was ill at the time, so when the bell was tolled it would be known who had died. The bells were also used as a curfew which were rung at 8pm each winter night. There was also a joyful peal at weddings. Brother Jack Woodford was one of the bellringers.

Buses did not run to the village for many years. Passengers had to walk to Brickworth corner to catch the bus.

Vera Fortune in Post Office 1986 just before her retirement

CHAPTER 5

FARMING THROUGH THE CENTURY

Without going into the historical background it is difficult to describe farming as it was in the Parish of Whiteparish in 1900 compared with 2000. The final enclosures of land were made around 1825. The politics of the time, the recent war with the French and an increase in the population of Britain were the principal causes. Grain prices had increased dramatically, and the Landlords of the time were pushed to plough up as much land as possible, good or poor. However a large section of the poorer land of the parish was still left as common land with many cottagers holding rights to grazing and firewood. In 1900 many householders in the parish still held common rights. The Common exists to this day but in the intervening years up to 1999 many cottagers have lost their rights as they failed to register them. It was around 1965 that an Act of Parliament was brought in to make sure that those who wished to retain their rights could re-register. This was due to changing circumstances i.e. the increase in road traffic and the difficulties encountered when cattle roamed freely. A few folk have retained their rights, which can be found written into the deeds of the houses that were registered. In old terminology these common lands were called 'wastes'. Although the Lords of the Manors owned these 'wastes' they were powerless to stop the time-honoured rights of grazing and fuel collection. All that could be gained from the 'wastes' by the commoners was essential to them in what was a very harsh existence. However over a number of years small plots of land on the common were taken over by 'squatters' and hovels turned into houses. Often this was due to hard economic times, and the increase in population, forcing folk to find some place and land off which to live. The Lords of the Manor had to turn a blind eye to this practice or face an increasing number of starving folk causing trouble on their estates. In 1900 the Common of Whiteparish was still very important to the farmers on the smallholdings that had developed from those claimed by the squatters. They could run their cows on the Common and the small fields near their homes could be planted for hay and the growing of roots for winter-feeding. The Enclosure Act of Parliament, passed around 1825, contained clauses that made sure that small commoners were compensated. Giving them small parcels of land in lieu of their Common Rights did this. This was the practice in previous enclosures over the rest of the country where many new small landowners were tempted by money to sell to bigger landlords. However judging by the number of small farms in Whiteparish, this does not seem to have happened to any great extent. The 1895 Ordnance Survey map shows acreage of ground set aside for allotments for growing food that could be rented by villagers. This was probably due to the reduction over the years of the Common Land. It is within the memory of some parishioners that fodder roots could be seen growing on one or two allotments to help feed the cattle. Certainly the 'White Hart' public house ran a few cows and used the allotments in this way. Mrs Macphail whose maiden name was Hamblyn has recorded this fact in her taped memoirs. Again it is in the memory of the Woodford family of cows being kept at the 'Kings Head' public house and turned out onto the common well into the 1920s. Many small holdings shown on the Ordnance Survey map of 1892, farms hardly viable, needed the Common for grazing and the running of pigs in the acorn season (much as the New Forest commoners do today). The list of farmers and farms at the turn of the century, that we have managed to abstract from records, shows the pattern at the time remaining unchanged right up to the 1930s

Corn crops drying in the field in 'stooks'

Due to the cheap cereals, meat and dairy produce coming in from the Empire and Europe; British farming in the 1900s was in the middle of a deep depression. Farming methods of the middle to late 1800s, using rotation of crops and sheep folding up on the downlands could not compete in the market place. Gradually the trend was to sell fresh eggs, pork and milk, fed on the cheap imported grain. Fresh milk production for the growing populations of Southampton, Portsmouth and Salisbury other than the production of cheese and butter, which was coming from New Zealand, was what began to change the face of the countryside. This meant that sheep flocks and wheat fields up on the Whiteparish downs changed to poor rundown pasture and dairy cows. This change in the economy not only affected the farmers, the tenants of large estates but also the estates themselves, Lord Nelson to the West and South, Squire Lawrence and Miss Bristow to the North and East of the Parish. In Lord Nelson's case the change in the demand for timber by the ship building industry due to steel gradually replacing wood, combined with lower rents, made the estate unprofitable. The other two estates probably had larger private incomes to cushion the blow. Even here low rents and farm incomes from their inhand farms took the gilt off the gingerbread.

As far as we can ascertain, 28 farms in the parish were rented, four were over 150 acres in size, the rest varying from 2 acres up to 50. Rents per acre that were then paid are difficult to establish, but certainly not more than £1 per acre. Pheasant shooting, which had become very fashionable during the 1880s, was another factor in keeping the wolf from the landlord's door. It was the demand of the 'nouveau riche' whose money came from the thriving industrial areas of Britain that went a long way in saving the 'rurals' certainly in this parish. Many shooting agreements can be found in estate records relating to the woods and farms of the parish. The tenants had no say in these arrangements and certainly if caught poaching would have been turned out 'on their ear'. The positive sides to this was that the keepers and under keepers were employed, all adding to income within the parish, that had been lost by the decline of high farming. We cannot vouch for the story that one older resident gave us, when talking of these times. He recalls that a Mr. Albert Viney of Gills Hole farm (a very wet poor holding) applied for job of hangman for the area. We suppose today this would have been called diversification into a part time job! Perhaps an interesting story relating to shooting comes from Mr. Jack Woodford. His family, as can be gleaned from elsewhere in this book, were bakers and he can remember going round with his father before 1910 delivering bread. On one occasion he saw Lloyd George at Melchet Court with a shooting party. When asked how he knew this famous man he recalls the fact that his photograph was in the newspapers of the time, all due, no doubt, to Lloyd George's work in starting the welfare state. At the time this revolutionary idea, must have given a great deal of hope to folk in a poor parish like ours.

Early picture of a hayricks being built

The larger farms, which could feed bigger herds of cows, found an outlet for their milk in the surrounding towns. It was the railway station at Dean that was the key to these markets. A Salisbury dairyman had the foresight to build a creamery (now the parish hall at Dean) near the station and take milk from surrounding farms. That which was surplus to the liquid trade in the town he turned into butter or cheese, although it must have been a daunting task and very labour intensive. Another problem was delivering the dairy products to Dean a round trip of some 6 or 8 miles each day with only horses and carts available as transport. There was the advantage in that packages and parcels destined for Whiteparish and sent to Dean Railway station could be brought back to the village. We have set out below a list of farms in the parish around 1900 together with names of the farmers we have gleaned from records. The farms did not change much until after the World War of 1914 - 1918.

A common sight at the turn of the century

It was the 1914 - 1918 War that reinvigorated the agriculture of the country and of course the village for a time. Whereas after 1880 it was a case of 'up horn' 'down corn' from 1916 onwards it was the opposite, the German submarines saw to that. Farmers were reluctant to change course again, for they had seen during the years 1885 - 1905 those who had tried to carry on growing cereals become bankrupt. It was only when the Government, driven by the fear of mass starvation, made it compulsory to plough and sow again, did they respond. No doubt the first tractor might have come to the parish at this time (Ford of U.S.A.?) but as yet we have no evidence of this. By 1925 once again all this changed. Politics demanded the rug be pulled from the farming community, it was back to cheap food from the countries of the Empire, all of which were in desperate need of earning money to stave off their economic gloom. Back the parish went to cows and pigs with poultry. The demand for fresh food began to creep along, blasted for a while by the crash of the early 1930s. Our downlands reverted to rabbit warrens, bushes and ant hills. What grazing there was cost very little, for it was managed in the simplest way by the farmer, his dog and a stout stick. The number of farms began to decline due to amalgamation and tenants began to be offered the chance to buy their farms. Lord Nelson began to sell off parts of his estate that fringed upon this parish about 1925. In 1935 Squire Lawrence died and in May 1940 his estate was sold. More could be gained from investing in industry other than farming or forestry.

A ploughing match in the 1920s

Around 1900 the horse was the key to all rural and town transport. We have tried to work out the number of horses that may have been kept within the parish at this time. Our mathematics suggest around 120 - 150, some 100 heavy horses suitable for plough teams and heavy haulage e.g. timber and hay, the others used for delivery by the bakers and butchers and the very essential carrier. No doubt some of the bigger Public Houses in the parish had a pony and trap that could be used to bring or take passengers to the railway stations. This number of animals would have kept the four blacksmiths and the harness maker busy. The last harness maker in Whiteparish who has recently retired from the harness shop in the Street, is Mr Jack Hyde. (The shop was demolished a few years ago and houses have been built on the site). Riding and coaching horses were kept in the parish by at least three of the big houses and by the more affluent. To feed all these animals would, by our calculations, need some 400 acres of arable and pasture land.

Jack Hyde harness maker

By the 1920s some of these horses departed as the motor car began to take over. The number of blacksmiths declined or took on more general smithying. With the coming of World War 2 and the need for intense food production, farming mechanisation ousted the horse. However, if the work horse has declined over these years by 1999 horses for riding for pleasure have taken their place. In the last part of the century riding stables have been established in the village enabling the owners to earn a living by livery and teaching people to ride so that they may enjoy the excellent tracks and bridle ways that exist within the parish.

We have included, at this point, an extract from a small book compiled by school children at the village school in 1937, giving a very good idea of what life was like on the farms just before World War 2:-

"Most of the work done in the village is connected with farming in one way or another. Labourers, dairymen, shepherds do the actual farm work, but the harness maker, blacksmith, carpenter, hurdle maker and thatcher all do their share of work connected with the farm. As he is not thatching the whole year round, the thatcher usually does other work as well. His work will be different according to the time of the year, but he is a useful man because he can turn his hand to almost any kind of farm work. Dairy farming is the chief kind of farming done in the district. Although some butter is made and sold in the village, most of the milk is collected by lorries belonging to the United Dairies and taken to either Salisbury or Southampton. Several small farms sell their milk within the village. Where butter is made the skimmed milk is used to keep pigs, some of which are taken to Salisbury market to be sold while they are still small. Others are fattened, either for pork or bacon. If pork, the local butcher can use them. Some of the bacon pigs are now sent to Downton bacon factory. Calves and cows that are to be sold are taken to Salisbury market by lorries.

Sheep are kept by a few farmers, but sheep-rearing is not as important as dairy-farming. The sheep are of the South Down breed and sold for mutton. There is one large poultry farm in the parish but every farmer, and many other people too, keep fowls. Many eggs are used at home or sold locally, but a dealer comes round every week to buy those that are not needed in Whiteparish.

Hay fields are laid up each spring to provide animal feed during the winter, also swedes, turnips and mangolds are grown. These root crops are put into heaps and covered with straw to keep out the frost and fed to cows during the winter. Wheat, oats and barley are grown and corn sheaves are stacked in ricks to be threshed during the winter, and the straw used for thatching and bedding cattle during the winter. Almost every farm has its own orchard, where apples of every kind and some pears and plums are grown. A few people use their fallen apples to make cider. One farmer has a cider press and lends it to others when he has finished pressing his apples"

The story of farming within the parish during the last war can easily be told. It was a desperate rush from the 'up horn' of before 1939 to 'up corn', and much of the downland was ploughed up and quite a lot of old pasture on the poorer farms. The farmers in this area, like their fellows elsewhere, were compelled by the war agricultural committees to do as ordered or be turned out of the farm. Whiteparish had a role to play in improving the fertility of the soil for many miles around at this time. Chalk from the quarry at Pepperbox was used to sweeten the acid soils of the surrounding farms that had been neglected since the depression. It was by no means easy to change from looking after cows to growing wheat and potatoes. Many had forgotten the techniques involved and found it very difficult to find and use ploughs and cultivating equipment. Mr Stride (who farmed Goldens farm) recalls having to grow an acre of potatoes on his holding as well as fodder and cereal for his cows as the cheap imports of the 1930s of grain and protein ceased almost overnight. Growing potatoes meant a great deal of hard work, not only to plant but also to harvest. Weeds had to be killed by hoeing, a back breaking task, as those of the older generation can well remember. In his case, his father was at that time an invalid, so he was exempted from being called up for the forces as there was no one else to run the farm. Mr Angel, who farms at Cowesfield was called up, but had to return to the farm to help out, as his father was not a fit man and the work load was increasing by leaps and bounds.

Cider making has been a popular pastime throughout the century

Unlike the first war the need for food was world wide, certainly in Europe, which meant that farming was forced to keep on expanding its output well into the 1950s. From this point farming became fully mechanised and Whiteparish farmers took advantage of all new methods on offer. One example was the Artificial Insemination bull stud farm started in the New Forest. Thus the improvement of the milk potential of the village cows was increased year on year due to the availability of top line sires at stud, something a small farmer could not have afforded on his own. Both Mr Stride and Mr Andrews recall being the last folk to hand milk their cows and only bought their milking machines around 1960.

Today there are only five milk producers left milking between them some three hundred cows. The other 25 producers that existed around 1900 gradually gave up as farms amalgamated for economic reasons. Both Mr Stride and the late Mr Andrews have retired from active farming and sold or let their land for others to work. The downland is now intensively farmed, arable, much of it by the Parsons family whose grandfather was active back in 1900.

*Lorries with milk churns. This type of lorry is typical of those used by
Mr Dear to transport milk*

Mr Parsons harvesting wheat on land north of the A27 looking towards Whelpley Farm

We list below the farms and farmers who were active in the early part of this century. It would be interesting to compare the labour employed in the parish in 1900 with that of today. Unfortunately we have not got access to the census figures of the past 100 years, the last available was 1895. Details will not be published until 100 years have elapsed from the date of each census and will make interesting reading.

Farms and Farmers 1900 - 1920 taken from Kelly's Directory.

John & Albert Andrews - Redhill Farm.
George Fulford - Dairy House Farm (1919).
Alfred & Edward Gay - Alderstone House Farm (over 150 acres).
Charles Hatcher - Common Farm.
Jeremiah & Alexander Hayter - Morrisholt Farm.
Thomas Snelgar - Whites Farm.
John Snook - Newton & Whelpley Farm.

Mr James Stride, Mrs Annie Stride, Mrs Fanny Stride - Goldens Farm.
Fred Walters - Moor & Tichbourne Farm (over 150 acres).
Frank Frith, John Frith - Chadwell Farm.
Jesse Hayes - Barters Farm.
Albert Viney - Gills Hole Farm.
William Courtney Page - Baker, Grocer & Farmer - Blaxwell, Street, Chalkpit Farm.
Also clerk to Parish Council.
Victor Parsons - Brickworth & Whelpley Farm.
Stephen Newton Webb - Old Manor Farm.
Frank Slade - Dairy House Farm (1920)
Henry Walter Light - Hawthorns - Smallholder.

Listed but no farms given.

Richard Wallace 1911	Henry Dunn 1907 - 1911	James Pile - 1902
Lawrence Molesworthy 1911	Frank Newman - 1903	Charles Dredge - 1903
William Holloway 1907 -		

Typical price paid for a house.

Lion House   £150 (1925)

Typical price paid for a farm.

Andrews Farm   £400 (Circa 1920)

Sale of Cowesfield Estate in March 1940.

An Estate of 1689 Acres sold by Knight Frank & Rutley

Rents of tenanted farms

Home Farm £165 per annum (124 acres)
Dairy House Farm £130 p.a. (100 acres)
Rowden Farm £189 p.a. (215 acres)
Lower Cowesfield Farm £220 (171 acres)
Manor Farm, Cowesfield Green £105 (37 acres)
Bushy Farm £68 (27 acres)
Yew Tree Farm £60 (21 acres)
Holloway Farm £23 (10 acres)

Cottages, Rent per annum

Frogmore Cottage & Land 4.5 acres	£17 10s
Sunnyside, Cowesfield Green 0.3 acres	£8 5s.
74 Bungalow, Cowesfield Green 0.189 acres	£20 16s
Woodside Cottage 0.25 acres	£10
Manor Cottage, Cowesfield Green 0.13 acres	£14.
No1 Rose Mead Cottage 0.18 acres	£12
No 1 Testwood Cottage 0.41 acres	£10
Garden Bothy House	£7 4s

Sporting Rights £275 per annum

CHAPTER 6

FARMING MEMORIES RECORDED OVER THE PAST TWO YEARS

Bill Angel of Home Farm, Cowesfield.

Bill Angel 1999

Bill Angel's experience of farming started in 1931when he was 12 years old when his father rented a farm. There were about 12 'holdings', rather than farms on the Cowesfield Estate. They farmed about 160 acres, which was quite a large farm for those days. Rent was about £1 per acre. Mr Angel was a tenant of Lord Lawrence. Mr (Squire) Lawrence who owned the land originally died in 1935 and his widow remarried Lord Lawrence, and soon after her death the Estate was split up.

The farm was a dairy farm of 25 Shorthorn cows all milked by hand. The milk was sent to United Dairies. When the Milk Marketing Board was brought in things became much easier as regular cheques came in. They also grew a little barley and had a team of horses, 2 working and 1 resting. Also kept a few pigs.

Bill Angel was supposed to do Military Training but was called back during haymaking when his father was not well, and he had all the farming work on his shoulders so in fact he never did any Military Training.

During the war farmers were told to plough as much as possible and that in Mr Angel's opinion is why there is all the trouble with the 'right to roam'. The Downland, which had been open land, became fields of crops or was used to graze sheep.

They bought their first tractor in 1939 and the hired hand was no longer needed. During the war they often had help from the army. Mr Angel remembers the problems of fencing cows with only barbed wire as fencing.

Bill Angel joined Sherfield English Home Guard, which met in the village hall. Life at that time was very tiring when a night on duty was followed by a full day's work on the farm, which involved milking a herd of 20 - 25 cows. They bought their first milking machine in 1948. Eventually Mr Angel bought the farm in 1952 or 53 and ran it with one hired hand. The number of cows increased. The farm income has suffered during the B S E crisis but he remembers worse times in the 1930's when the farm often had to manage without cow-cake and swedes had to be grown as fodder.

After 1945 when milk was in demand, he began to cross his Shorthorns with Friesians and later Holsteins were used. He also had Guernsey cows for their cream, which was in demand.

Mr & Mrs Angel have kept the farm going for the next generation.

Home Farm, Cowesfield

Mr and Mrs Stride of Goldens Farm

Grandmother, a widow with seven children, held a tenancy at the turn of the century from Lord Nelson, who, was thought to be a kindly landlord. Father bought the farm in 1924 for, it is thought, £1,700. The farm had been 53 acres in size and rented for £1 per acre, but at the time of the sale a small portion of 13 acres had already been sold off. It was a dairy farm and by the time Mr Stride, an only child, was old enough to work with his father the farm had 15 or 16 cows, 100 to 200 hens and a few pigs. The farm owners had Common Rights in Whiteparish. Cows would run on the Common but although the Strides still have Common Rights they have not taken advantage of it, as there are problems with the cows on the roads and in gardens. Mr Stride took over from his father in 1945 and to this day he and his wife have exercised their 'fuelling rights' as Commoners.

Before the Milk Marketing Board was formed milk was sent to a dairy concern in Southampton which eventually became Nestles and subsequently United Dairies. Nestles were generous towards their farmers, giving chocolates as presents at Christmas.

Milking was done by hand, Mr Stride's father did not like machinery, he still had horses and carts. Milk in his day was being sold for six old pennies a quart and later six old pennies for a gallon. Things were very difficult but most small farmers did not pay rates or Income Tax.

During the 1939 - 1945 war things improved somewhat but there were still many restrictions on what farmers could or could not produce.

In 1960 when Mr Stride, senior, died the farm was brought more up to date.

Goldens Farm 1999

Miss Andrews and the late Mr Andrews Of Cottage Farm

Mr and Miss Andrew's father lived in and worked a family farm, Redhill Farm, on the other side of the A36. When he married he moved into the village in 1915. The farm was 50 acres, the average size of a farm in Whiteparish, which made a fair living though no one ever got rich. The rent was paid to the Nelson Estate. Father bought the farm in the early 1920's. It was basically a dairy farm, butter being made from the milk and sold locally. Hens and a pig were kept. Father farmed alone with hired local help at busy times. They ran a herd of 12 cows to start with, which gradually increased to 30.

Len and Marjory Andrews in the 1920s in front of their farm home

They were relieved when the Milk Marketing Board was founded in 1933 and a fair price could be obtained for milk. Before that farmers had to find their own contracts to sell milk or butter. The farm was run without tractors, the family was not mechanically minded, and also tractors did not seem to be reliable enough. The land was heavy clay, which was difficult to manage, "not boys land" it used to be said.

Both Mr and Miss Andrews went to school in the village. Mr Andrews stayed on the farm to help father, farming through the depression of 1929 when value of stock etc. was halved.

Brother Leonard (Mr Andrews) retired entirely from the farm in 1989. The milking was done by machine. The cows could not run on the clay fields in winter. The farm started with Shorthorn cattle but changed to Freisians in the 1940's for milk better suited for butter. Father and son managed the farm, with mother in the background. Miss Andrews went away to work but came back to help out on the farm when her mother died as the farm could not afford a hired hand. They sold Bramley apples by the bushel from their orchard, which is now 'The Bramleys'. The farm was fertilised with natural products, no artificial fertilisers. The farm had a telephone fairly early otherwise it meant riding on a bike into the village to make phone calls

Mr Andrews and Miss Andrews did not take advantage of their 'common rights' in Whiteparish for fear of their animals being a nuisance to others. They can remember forest ponies wandering in the village area. There was a pond in the village in Common Road near Pondside cottage.

Miss Andrews, as a child, recalled that poor pensioners drew their 10/- a week pension but with 2/- for rent, a bit for coal, they had nothing left for clothes. They seemed to wear the same clothes summer and winter. She can recall various cottages dotted around the village, many thatched, which were wonderfully warm in winter and cool in summer but a terrible fire risk

Miss Andrews recalls the poverty in the village. Children with very poor shoes and always looking half-starved but it made people tough. There was not a lot of casual work and any work had to be competed for.

CHAPTER 7

PLACES OF WORSHIP
IN WHITEPARISH
1900 - 2000

Between 1900 and 1914 there were five places of worship in the village, All Saints Church - Anglican, the Wesleyan Chapel, a Primitive Methodist Chapel in Clay Street, a Plymouth Brethren meeting house in Common Road next to Wayside Cottage now called 'The Bungalow' and another in the property next to the Fountain Inn now called the 'Cottage'.

At the end of this century there are just two places of worship, the Anglican Church and the Methodists' Chapel both with well supported congregations.

All Saints Church, the early years

As far as All Saints Church is concerned we have been unable to find any change to the fabric of the building until well into the century. In 1900 there is a report of the need to buy a bier and it is understood that the resulting 'buy' was in the old vicarage stables (Garage) for many years.

In 1902 there was a special Thanksgiving for Peace following the Boer War and a collection was made of £2 7s 0d, no reference was made to whom the donation was given. In 1908 there is a mention of bringing up to date the heating arrangements in the church. In the same year a Sunday School Clothing Club was set up in which a penny a week per child could be saved, and if at the end of the year a regular amount had been saved all year, a bonus would be added to the child's account. By 1914 a sum of £19 14s 3d (£19.71p) had been saved and the bonus (paid by the vicar) was £1 19s 0d (£1.45p) which prompted the vicar to ask for financial assistance.

An aerial view of All Saints Church in the 1960s

Not a lot is on record as having changed for many years, although the Church Clock has been a problem over the years, it was silent during the War Years and was eventually repaired, cleaned and oiled in 1955 at a cost of £11. In October 1969 a peal of 5040 changes was rung, the peal called 'Plain Bob Minor' took one hour fifty four minutes to ring. For a period the village had a clock striking the hours but by 1972 the clock had to be dismantled, cleaned and repaired once again. The clock was put in place with great ceremony in 1975. In July 1977 a driving cable broke which was repaired and re-installed with the help of the vicar at the time, the Rev Keeley. Following the re-installing of the clock, one of the hands fell off, it had corroded badly, and a local man, Mr Jury, made a new set of fibreglass hands. In 1998 an electronic set of bells were installed and at the same time a chiming clock was introduced once more. The hours and half-hours are now struck during the daylight hours.

In 1967 the first 'festival of Flowers and Music' was held followed by a second Festival in 1977.

Donations have been given to the church over the years in memory of parishioners. £100 was given to the Vestry Fund in 1968, a new lectern and bible in 1978 and in

1979 a new medallion window was donated. The church was rewired in 1988 following an anonymous donation and in the same year the church received a new communion rail and a new cross and candlestick.

In February 1970 the new vestry was dedicated and blessed by the Ven. S B Wingfield Digby and in the same year members of the village worked new kneelers and Mrs Fenwick designed a new frontal for the high altar. In 1987 a new altar was designed in memory of the Rev Roger Keeley who died whilst in office here in Whiteparish

Inside the church, schoolchildren taking part in the 150th anniversary of the opening of the school

Children parading outside the church during the schools 150th anniversary

1996 saw the old organ removed and another bought from Chudleigh U R C. It was restored, enlarged and moved to Whiteparish. There is a plaque on the organ commemorating Mrs Kathleen Hayes who died in 1985, she was organist in the church for more than 50 years. In 1999 there are moves afoot to provide new kneelers for the North Aisle.

The history of the Methodist Chapel in the village during the 100 years this book is covering is equally as interesting. It has been renowned for its singing and for its teas at Harvest Festivals and other anniversaries. Early in the century in 1903 the schoolroom, Vestry and Kitchen were built and in 1906 a new Harmonium was bought. In 1926 Mr Alford, the carpenter, was asked to make eight new trestle tables which were bought for £4 10/- (£4.50) and are probably the ones still in use in the village to this day. In 1937 the Chapel was registered to consecrate marriages and the second couple to marry, Mr and Mrs Ralph Elkins, still reside in the village.

Mrs Kathleen Hayes sitting at the old organ in Whiteparish Church'

In 1940 mains electricity was installed but not until 1957 was mains water brought into the Chapel rooms. The car parking area was paved, so that the life of the congregation and visiting preachers was made easier. In 1970 a modern W. C. was installed and at last the Elsan bucket could be removed. In 1972 the heating was updated in the schoolroom using Electric Fan Heaters, and new chairs replaced the swing back forms. In 1973 the Chapel was refurbished, pews being replaced by chairs and the temperamental old stove was replaced by oil filled radiators. The stove had been known to blow open its doors with a mighty bang and was at times red-hot.

An organ replaced the early harmonium in 1985. In 1994 a loop system was installed to enable the hard

The Methodist Chapel 1999

of hearing to enjoy the services and in 1995/6 the Chapel was carpeted and handrails fitted to make entry into the Chapel much easier. The kitchen and toilets have recently been redecorated.

The Chapel and its congregation support many good causes most generously. Harvest Festivals and Carol Services boost donations to charities, the World Relief Fund, the 'Seaman's Mission', the National Children's' Homes, Homes for the Aged, and holidays for under privileged children are just a few of the many.

The Ladies Bright Hour meetings started in 1948 and some of the founder members are still attending meetings.

Sunday school Outings has for many years been an exciting day for the children, in early days a wagon trip to Nomansland or Pepperbox Hill but more recently a trip to the seaside when two motor coaches would leave filled with children, parents and friends.

The Anglican Church and the Methodists Chapel have for several years shared services once a month, alternating venues and both Church and Chapel welcome visitors to their services or just to look around the buildings.

A modern day service 'the blessing of the pets of the village'.
The Rev Marion Clutterbuck in centre 1999

CHAPTER 8

THE VICARS AND THE VICARAGE

We have been unable to find evidence that the start of the year 1900 was celebrated in Whiteparish possibly because the country was in the throes of the Boer War, which at that time was not progressing well. The fence round the church had just been replaced by an attractive wall built by Romany Chalk, bricklayer, assisted by the butcher's boy who became father of Mr Beauchamp. The curfew bell was still being rung for 5 to 10 minutes at 8pm each evening from 5th November until St. Valentines day (14th February) with a fortnights break at Christmas. It is said that Squire Lawrence having lost his way in the woods and having been guided home by the bell paid the bell ringers for the rest of his lifetime. The practice of ringing the curfew was discontinued during the 1st World War.

The vicar at All Saints Church in 1900 was the Rev. J C James who had been Vicar since 1897. He left the village for Winkleigh in 1902 and was succeeded by Charles Frederick Metcalfe who served Whiteparish for 14 years. Society at that time was stratified in a way, which would be inconceivable today. Contact was maintained between the social strata provided suitable deference was shown to the more elevated. The vicar, like other clergy, was in the privileged position of being able to maintain unreserved social contact with all parishioners. The doctor was probably the only other Whiteparish resident who had the same easy relationship with everybody. Parishioners and others visiting the Vicarage called either at the front door or the back door according to their social status. For example back door visitors included the carrier who called once a week for shopping orders from Salisbury, and all tradesmen. Visitors such as Squire Lawrence, the doctor, the schoolmaster and other social callers came to the front door.

The Vicarage in Rev. Metcalfe's time originated from two back to back cottages with a drawing room and bedroom above built onto the south end. This additional part had a higher roof than the part originating from the two cottages and was demolished when the new vicarage was built.

The front door was approached by a carriage drive from the front gate. To the right of the front door was a large stone, which had previously been used for mounting horses. A turn to the right on entering the front gate led to a coach house, with a hayloft above. Beyond the coach house, which subsequently became a garage, was a stable where a pony named "Peggy" was housed. Beyond the stable was a yard in which there was a large pit for the accumulation of manure for the garden provided by "Peggy". In the same yard were a store for fire logs, an apple house and a carpenter's workshop.

An early photograph of the old vicarage, showing on the left, the Victorian extension removed when the new vicarage was built

The old vicarage, now a private house, with the extension removed

The garden was extensive as it included land on which separate houses have since been built. At the time of Rev Metcalfe's residence it included two apple orchards, a tennis court, several herbaceous flower borders and two glasshouses.

Near the back door of the vicarage was a well, which provided water for domestic use when the rainwater supply failed during the summer. The water from the well was placed in a 100-gallon tank from where it was released via a tap into a water storage tank under the vicarage scullery floor. The water from the well was not fit for drinking and potable water had to be obtained from the well at the back of the Fountain Inn. The drinking water was stored in the larder and was passed through a "Pasteur" filter before it could be consumed.

The inmates of the vicarage at this time consisted of the Rev and Mrs Metcalfe, their two sons, a maid of all work, whose activities were supplemented by a visiting charlady, and a nanny. A wholetime gardener named Alford who received 15/- a week largely maintained the garden. (Alford's two brothers were the village carpenters who had a workshop opposite the end of Newton Lane) Besides tending the garden Alford also pumped out the cesspool every day and the contents were taken in a handcart for distribution in the orchard. This produced magnificent crops of apples and a nauseating smell, which was not popular with the neighbours.

In 1910 the vicar bought a car, a single cylinder, 6-horse power Rover, its average speed was about 16 miles per hour. This car superseded the dogcart, which up to then had been the usual means of transport.

It was in 1910 that Edward V11 died and the village was informed by the tolling of the church bell. This was followed in 1911 by a celebration of the coronation of George V which was marked by a festive lunch in a large tent made of sailcloth erected in the field next to the vicarage (there were no houses on this section of the east side of Common Road at that time). Sweets were distributed to children from a shepherd's hut in the same field.

Sunday at the vicarage started with the Vicar and Mrs Metcalfe getting up for the 8am-communion service. After breakfast the Metcalfes assembled in the dining room at about 10am while the three bells in the church were rung by Mr Beauchamp, Mr Tubb and one other. At 10.55am a single bell was rung by Mr Beauchamp for 5 minutes while the Vicar, adorned in frock coat and Noahs Ark hat led his family to the church, the maid and nanny remaining in the vicarage to prepare the lunch (they had to go to Evensong at 6.30pm).

In the church most members of the congregation had their allotted places. Squire Lawrence and his wife sat at the front just below the pulpit. Behind the Lawrences sat the Anstells, the vicarage family a little further back, while Capt. Davis and his family occupied a pew near the front of the north aisle. The organ was played by Mr Lockyer and a small boy pumped the bellows. Mr Faulkner, the Schoolmaster, read the Lessons

In 1914 when the First World War started, Whiteparish, like the rest of the country, was faced with numerous stresses and problems. First there was the call up and general rush to join the army. Those left at home had to face new problems. One that affected life at the vicarage was the arrival of refugees from Belgium. Two groups were assigned to Whiteparish. One consisted of a number of women peasants from an agricultural community, whose menfolk were presumably in the Belgian Army. These ladies were housed in a farm near Brickworth and used to catch large numbers of sparrows under sieves supported by sticks, the sparrows being attracted by a sprinkling of breadcrumbs. Strings attached to the sticks were pulled causing the sieves to fall and trap the birds. Many of the resulting corpses were brought to the vicarage at Christmas, a gift that had to be tactfully discouraged.

The second group of refugees, one family, was installed in a cottage near Newton Corner. The husband was a diamond cutter. Special newspapers, in French, were published for the refugees and it was the Vicar's responsibility to distribute them.

The Rev Metcalfe left Whiteparish in 1916 and details of what happened in and around the vicarage under the new and subsequent Vicars is not recorded in such detail. He was replaced after a short break by the Rev W P Arden who was the first of many Whiteparish Vicars who had served or were trained in countries other than the United Kingdom. The Rev Arden served in British Columbia and became Chaplain to the forces in Malta. He was succeeded in 1926 by the Rev W P Hughes who although trained in the United Kingdom had served the past 10 years in New Zealand. He was in Whiteparish for only one year when he was appointed Chaplain to the RAF in Aboukir. In 1940 the Rev F J Tozer came to Whiteparish, he had served in Ladysmith, Natal and in 1945 the village gained the services of the Rev B C D Palmer who had trained and served in New Zealand. In 1951 we were joined by another interesting appointment; the Rev B N Carver who had been Chaplain to the Royal Navy from 1919-1938 and Hon Chaplain to H M King George VI from 1942-46. The last of the Vicars, who had served abroad, other than the current Vicar, was the Rev E T Mackie who joined us in 1963 after serving in the Falkland Islands and Chile

The new vicarage

Vicars of Whiteparish 1900 - 2000

Rev J.C.James	1987 - 1902	Rev B.N.Carver	1951
Rev C.F.Metcalfe	1902	Rev E.T.Mackie	1963
Rev W.P.Arden	1916	Rev R.Keeley	1968
Rev W.P.Hughes	1926	Rev D.C.Gooderham	1987
Rev J.C.Rendell	1927	Rev B.Skelding	1991
Rev W.Grace	1929	Rev Hazel Skelding	1994
Rev F.J.Tozer	1940	Rev Marion Clutterbuck	1996
Rev B.D.C.Palmer	1945		

CHAPTER 9

EXTRACTS FROM WHITEPARISH & LANDFORD CHURCH MONTHLY 1900-1910

August 1900

The Whiteparish Court of the Ancient Order of Foresters (A.O.F). held their annual Fete on July 18th. The new handsome banner recently purchased was used for the first time. A fair number of members attended Service, and afterwards, joined by visitors, dined at the 'White Hart'. After dinner letters from Mr Lawrence, Mr Archibald Morrison, and Mr Spark, regretting their absence, were read, and loyal and other toasts were drunk. The Secretary's statement as to funds and strength of membership gave, it is believed, every satisfaction.

In the afternoon a clown cricket match was played, and dancing and other amusements were enjoyed in the 'White Hart' meadow till dark.

A movement is on foot for the purchase of a Bier for the use in the parish (Whiteparish). There

The 'White Hart' meadow, the land rented by the landlord of the 'White Hart', now the Memorial Ground

can be no question as to the need, or at least the desirability, of one. It would cost from £7 to £10, probably. A subscription list will be placed at the Post Office, or contributions may be handed to Mr Woodford, Mr Till, Mr Foote or Mr Gill, who have kindly consented to help the matter forward.

September 1901

The Vicar, who has heard no Whiteparish News to enable him to give an account of Parish events, prints this month the following notes on 'His Fourth Leg' copied from the St. James's Gazette of August 16th 1901.

His Fourth Leg - A young British Officer at the front recently wrote home to his father from South Africa:- "Dear father, kindly send me £50 at once; lost another leg in a stiff engagement, and am in hospital without means" - The answer was:- "My Dear Son, - As this is the fourth leg you have lost, according to your letters, you ought to be accustomed to it by this time. Try to wobble along on any of the others you have left."

Postscript - The Quoit Club lately formed at Whiteparish have played three matches already and have won two of them.

A match against Romsey was won by 36 points, and of two played against Downton (a crack side), one was won by 5 points, and the other lost by 25 points.

August 1902

June 15th - Peace Thank Offerings were made at the Parish Church Services, and were supplemented by subscriptions sent to the Vicar subsequently. The amount collected was £2 7s. for Soldiers Widows and Orphans, and £1 5s. for the S.P.G.

June 13th - George Hayter, aged 91, the oldest man in the parish, was called to rest after a short illness. His funeral was largely attended by parishioners and friends from Salisbury, by all of whom he was held in high esteem for his blameless life of simple piety.

June 24th - Consternation and dismay filled the minds of all when the sad news of the King's illness reached the parish. On the morning of June 26th it was decided by the committee that it would be better to carry out the Coronation festivities, without any Coronation, in a modified degree. The processions, torchlight and other, and bonfire were postponed. Divine Service was well attended. It was a service of intercession for the life and recovery of the King. Hymns 375, 373 and 165, and the National Anthem were sung, the first two prayers in the service for the Visitation of the Sick were said, and the Vicar said a few words from the pulpit. At 1 pm between 500 and 600 sat down to dinner in an excellent, spacious tent, skilfully erected by Mr Foote, Mr Martin, and others. During the afternoon some of the sports' competitions took place. Directly after tea the volumes of smoke seen told of the unfortunate fire at Mr Lawrence's stables, and in a very short time practically the whole parish were at the scene, many hands doing all they could to save what was not already burning. Later in the evening there was dancing. Special thanks are due from all of us to Mr A Gay for the kind loan of his field, and to the committee for the admirable arrangements for the dinner and tea, and to many others.

Cricket - On July 5th our Club were beaten by East Tytherley by 89 runs to 53. Mr Faulkner batted in his old style.

On Sunday, July 13th, the Vicar announced that he has been offered and has accepted the Curacy of Winkleigh, in North Devon. He will leave to take up work there at the beginning of October. He will be sorry to sever ties and attachments formed in the parish and neighbourhood during his five years' Vicariate, but hopes that all will pray to God with him to send a pastor, who, with less shortcomings and failings, will far, far more than fill his place.

Organ Fund.- The proposed sale in aid of this will be held in the Schoolroom at the end of September. Fuller notice will be given. Mrs James hopes that all who have so kindly helped before, and fresh volunteers, will be getting ready by making and collecting any saleable articles, old and new.

January 1903

The Schools - The Rev F E Skyrme visited the Schools on November 13th and examined the children in religious knowledge. He reports as follows :-

"The School is in excellent order and shows careful and reverent teaching in all religious subjects of the syllabus".

Mr Hicks, the Government Inspector, paid one of his surprise visits on December 11th. He appeared well satisfied with the progress being made.

Football - The results of the football matches have been -

Whiteparish v Landford a win 1 - 0
"   v Bartley   a loss 3 - 0
"   v Wellow   a win 2 - 0

Entertainment - The Whiteparish Minstrals gave an Entertainment in the Schoolroom on Friday evening, November 28th. There was a fair company present, who enjoyed the fare, in the way of jokes, songs and sketches, provided for them. The Entertainment was repeated at Dean on Friday, December 12th, where the attendance was not so satisfactory.

June 1906

MEETING TO DISCUSS THE EDUCATION BILL. A very well attended meeting was held at the School on Friday, May 18TH, over 80 being present. The Chair was taken by the Right Hon. The Earl Nelson, supported by W F Lawrence and the Vicar. The general tone evidenced at the meeting was that of a wish for peace and a settlement on an equitable basis. There was an unanimous opinion that Religious Education should be retained in the Schools. That this is not impossible in practice was shown by the Chairman, who, referring to his long connection with the Whiteparish Schools, said he had never during the whole time heard a single word of complaint, or a single suggestion of unfairness, in regard to the teaching of the

Diocesan Syllabus. After the Vicar, Mr Lawrence and Mr Lampard had addressed the meeting, the following resolutions were agreed to by the large majority of those present, no one voting against them:-

1. That the voluntary system should in some form be retained, and the rights of the Trusts respected.
2. That all religious teaching should be given in compulsory school hours, and that some religious instruction should be universally provided.
3. That opportunity for denominational teaching should be given in all schools alike.
4. That teachers should have liberty to give such denominational teaching in all schools.
5. That some security for religious belief should be required in the case of every teacher authorised to give religious instruction.
6. That the right of parents to have their children taught the religion they desire should be recognised.
7. That the powers of the proposed Commission should be restricted, and the right of appeal to the High Court provided.

At the conclusion a hearty vote of thanks was recorded to the Chairman, on the motion of Mr Lawrence, seconded by Mr Spark, the latter dwelling in feeling terms upon the great sympathy and earnestness with which his Lordship had approached the question, and suggesting that if all would work together in the same spirit, there would not be long to wait for a peaceable settlement.

THE LIBRARY - We wish to call the attention of our readers to the fact that the second half year commences with July, and that for a very modest sum of threepence, they can enjoy a very good selection of books that will carry them well through the six months. The Library is open at the Reading Room on the first and third Mondays in each month from 12 to 1 pm.

THE CHURCH PLATE - It may not be generally known that there is a very handsome silver flagon and dish belonging to the Church. These were presented to the Church in 1671, and were the gift of Edward St. Barbe and Mary his wife, who formerly lived at the old Manor House, which stood in what is now known as 'The new Churchyard'. The Vicar will be pleased at any time to show these most interesting pieces of plate to any of the Parishioners who would care to see them.

The Vicar proposes taking his holiday during July. Mr White, who kindly filled his place two years ago, has undertaken the work again. He will be staying at the King's Head, and all parochial matters should be referred to him at that address. All applications for Infirmary Tickets during the Vicar's absence should be made to Mr. Faulkner.

February 1907

Jumble Sale - Christmas week witnessed one of the now famous Jumble Sales, and we believe that those that came for bargains were pleased with what they secured. Mrs Llewellyn, Mrs Metcalfe, the Misses Llewellyn, Spare, and Zebedee, and Mr

Faulkner, made most energetic stallholders, and as a result of their day's shopkeeping they made a sum of over £5, which has been slightly added to by subsequent sales. When the full amount is to hand, it will be given in aid of the Choir Stalls.

June 1908

The Vestry - The Easter Vestry was held on Friday evening April 24th. In the absence of the Vicar, the Rev C H Gould presided, and there was a greater number present than is usually the case. The accounts for the last year were presented and passed, and the Vicar nominated Mr Jesse Hayes as his Churchwarden. Interest centred round the heating arrangements of the Church, which need renewing, and it was decided to procure estimates for a system of heating the Church with hot water, as being more satisfactory and more economical. The improvement of the Choir Stalls, for which some funds have been contributed, also came in for its share of attention, and both matters will again be discussed at a meeting to be called at a later date.

The Snow Storm - It seems strange and almost incredible, with the sun brightly shining, the birds singing, the trees in green leaf, to think that, less than a month ago, Whiteparish experienced the greatest fall of snow it has known for years, and certainly the greatest that any of its inhabitants can remember so late in the spring. It commenced to fall early on Saturday morning, April 25th, and continued till about four in the afternoon. No Carriers from Whiteparish made their journey to Salisbury that day, no tradesmen made their accustomed rounds. A miller's van became imbedded in a drift in Newton Lane, and had to be dug out. The farmers were kept busy in their efforts to prevent their sheep and lambs from being buried in the snow. In the open there was a depth of 15 to 18 inches, while the drifts were of course much deeper. Fathers did the shopping that evening, and they followed the footsteps of the first to venture out. A frost followed the downfall, but on Sunday the sun shone brightly out and a thaw commenced and continued rapidly. Motorists coming up the Brickworth Road found it blocked, and on Monday it was found necessary to dig a way through, and also in the Newton Lane. Beyond the inconvenience, no great damage appears to have been done, but the storm will long be remembered in the Parish.

December 1908

Sunday school Clothing Club - It is proposed to start this club, in connection with the Morning Sunday school, at the beginning of the New Year. Any child attending the School will be entitled to join, paying a sum of not less than a penny a week. At the end of the year, those who have made a sufficient number of payments to secure it, will receive a bonus of one shilling. This Club will probably be found very useful to parents as a means of putting by something to help towards clothing their children. Where there are two or three children contributing, a nice little sum will be got together by the end of the year.

WHITEPARISH, LANDFORD and PLAITFORD PARISH MAGAZINE

May 1910

Easter Offering - The Vicar wishes to take this opportunity of thanking all those who contributed so generously towards the Easter Offering for the increase of the stipend of the living. It may not be generally understood that the shares purchased with this money from the Queen Victoria Clergy Sustentation Fund are not for the benefit of one particular incumbent, but for any Vicar who shall be Incumbent during any part of the year, so that, in the event of the death or resignation of any Vicar, his successor would receive a portion of the grant, from the time of his institution. It seems advisable to point this out, that parishioners may know that their offerings are for the benefit of the Stipend of the Living, and not for any particular Incumbent. It is also well that it should be known that the new scheme by which the Charity Commissioners are bringing up the Stipend of all Livings to a minimum of £200 a year does not apply to those Parishes where, like our own, the Patronage is in the hands of a private person.

Vestry Meeting - The annual Vestry was held on March 28th, at 7.30, when eleven persons were present. Mr Faulkner and Mr Tubb were appointed Churchwardens, and Mr Viney and Mr Fulford as Sidesmen. The Churchwardens' and Fabric Fund Accounts were presented, and duly audited as correct. The Churchwardens desired the Vicar to point out that all wreaths, glass cases &c., placed on graves in the Churchyard were so placed at the owners' risk, and, while all care would be taken of them, the Vicar and Churchwardens could not be responsible for any damage that might be done to them. We would be very glad to welcome more parishioners at the Vestry Meeting, for sometimes complaints are raised of decisions arrived at by the Vestry, which complaints would be much better brought forward at the time than afterwards, when the criticism, however excellent, cannot be acted upon.

CHAPTER 10

EXTRACTS FROM THE MAGAZINE FOR THE RURAL DEANERY OF ALDERBURY 1912-1915

November 1912 - Whiteparish

Services of Thanksgiving for the Harvest were held on the Festival of St Michael and All Angels, the Church being tastefully decorated, and the offerings of fruit and vegetables for the use of Salisbury Infirmary very generous. We must thank all those who gave their time and abilities to the work of decoration. The collections throughout the day were for the Salisbury Infirmary, the amounts being as follows: Collections in Church, £6 13s 10d; Collections in Street, £2 17s 2d.

G F S - The working party for G F S members will be held from 6 to 8, the first meeting to be on Thursday, November 7th. Materials will be provided, but the members are requested to bring their own thimbles, needles and scissors. The proceeds from the sale of work will be given to the fund for providing day excursions in the country for children from the London slums.

Night School Outing - On September 14th the lads who attended the night school classes last winter spent a very pleasant day at Portsmouth with Mr Faulkner. They took train at Dean, and on their arrival inspected the gun wharf and armoury where they learnt something of modern weapons. Next a visit was paid to Nelson's "Victory, and then a trip made up the harbour to view the new floating dock recently placed there. By this time they were ready for dinner, after which they proceeded to the beach at Southsea to indulge in the pleasures of boating till the time came to make the return journey. The lads take the opportunity of thanking those gentlemen who kindly contributed towards the expense of their outing.

September 1913 - Evening Gardens at Whiteparish

The following is Mr Corbett's report presented to the County Agricultural Education Committee:

" The instruction had been given in a very satisfactory manner, the plots were clean, and the crops very good. Eight pupils had been admitted, but, owing to hay harvest, only three were present. The lads were much interested in their work, and their registration excellent."

December 1914

Clothing Club - The amount saved by the members of the Children's Sunday School Club totalled this year the respectable sum of £19 14s 3d. To this amount was added £1 9s 0d in bonuses. The Club has been running for five years, and during that time it has been the lot of the Vicar to provide the bonus. Will anyone share the privilege in the future?

Belgian Refugees - We have at last been able to welcome our first family of Refugees, and we are able to state that they are most comfortably housed at Whelpley. It is really a great pleasure to be able to help those brave people, they are so extremely grateful for everything that is done for them. The subscribers to their support may rest assured that their kindness is thoroughly appreciated. We hope shortly to accommodate another family in the house at Newton.

May 1915

Emergency Committee - A meeting of this Committee was held at the parish rooms on Easter Tuesday evening to receive a report of the work carried on by the Sub-Committee appointed to provide for the two Belgian families now the guests of the parish. It stated that two houses had been furnished by general contributions in kind, and that Mrs Ansdell had kindly supplied all the necessary utensils found wanting. The manner of catering was then given in detail, the weekly cost being about 30/- weekly for the two families, which would compare favourably with the expenses of other families in the immediate neighbourhood. The gratification of the Sub-Committee was expressed at the finding of the husband of Mrs Van Schil in hospital at Southampton, and through the kindness of Mr Spark and the Vicar she has been able to pay him a weekly visit and hopes were expressed that when the husband became convalescent we shall be able to welcome him as a further guest of the parish. The total income for 19 weeks has been £33 10s 6d and the total expenses £32 9s 1d. The General Committee expressed satisfaction at the report and recorded a vote of thanks to the Sub-Committee for the work they had done, and to which they have given much time and labour.

The War - Mr and Mrs Stone have heard from their son Walter that he is at present in one of the "rest" hospitals as he has been wounded, though fortunately not seriously, in the arm.

CHAPTER 11

THE COMING OF THE MOTOR CAR

From 'Memories of Whiteparish' 1904 - 1915 by
Charles Russell Metcalfe

During the time we lived at Whiteparish there were some major changes, one of the most significant being the introduction of the motor car. Before cars and lorries appeared on the scene the earlier horse drawn traffic ranged from brewers drays from Romsey (Strong's Romsey Ale) and Salisbury, farm carts and haywains to carriages of wealthy with coachmen and footman. There was also some steam traction engines with large metal wheels, which churned up the flint roads. Steam traction engines were used for various purposes ranging from work on farms to household removals. There were also steam engines drawn by horses, which were used to work threshing machines. This last type of vehicle always annoyed me because it seemed illogical to use horses to move steam engines. But then in those days horses were also used on the railways for moving goods trucks in shunting yards.

My father, the Vicar, had a dogcart for some years. Our dogcart had a seat for 2 looking towards the front of the vehicle, which was occupied by the driver and one passenger; there was a second seat for 2 facing backwards. A certain amount of luggage (or presumably some dogs) could be carried in a compartment between the front and back seats. There was no protection against the weather other than thick waterproof rugs and carriage umbrellas.

In 1910 when I was six years old, my father bought a single cylinder, 6 horse power Rover. This 2 seated vehicle cost more than £100 and it was delivered to Whiteparish from London at an additional charge of less than £1. Until recently I still had the receipt for this car. Its average speed was about 16 miles an hour and it reached Salisbury from Whiteparish in about 30 minutes, which was rapid compared with the carrier's carts, which took about 2 hours. The only other cars in the village at that time were the one belonging to Mr Sullivan at the King's Head and another belonging to Dr Case. Butcher Pearce's car was of a slightly later vintage. Also at about that time the Ansells came ostentatiously to All Saints Church in a Lanchester.

My father's Rover gradually became too small for the growing family and, at one stage it was customary to remove the door on the near side so that the passenger could sit on the floor with his feet resting on the running board. The car met with sundry adventures many of them caused by punctures or mechanical breakdowns. On one occasion it was driven backwards into a ditch from which it was extracted by 2 strong men. A particularly notable occasion was when my parents started on an expedition to Southampton to buy Sunday School prizes. One mile from the Vicarage the car came to a standstill and nothing would induce it to show any sign of life. So it returned ignominiously to the Vicarage drawn by a horse. The aid of Mr Sullivan was invoked and the entire engine was dismantled. I do not know precisely what was wrong but my father told me it was repaired by a wire nail, after which the engine was reassembled and normal running restored.

THE ROVER COMPANY LIMITED : COVENTRY

This car went through the Scottish Reliability Trials 1909, with highly satisfactory results

6 h.p. Rover Car

Three speeds, H.T. Magneto and accumulator and coil ignitions, high side doors, inside splashers to front guards, long foot boards, hood and screen.

Price, with hood & screen, £155   Without hood & screen, £140

Rover Detachable Wheels, including a fifth spare wheel, but no tyre, £8.10.0 extra per set (see page 22)

This Car is also supplied with wire wheels, 700 × 65 m m Dunlop tyres, with body upholstered in pegamoid, and platform back. No side doors, platform steps, hood or screen. Accumulator ignition only, at One Hundred Guineas.

N.B.—These prices include Dunlop tyres of the size specified at the prices current on November 1st, 1909. Any subsequent increase in the price of tyres will be charged extra.

After running the Rover for 3 years it was sold to somebody who transferred it to India. I often wonder what befell it in that country, but sadly I do not know.

Having disposed of the Rover my father acquired an "Alldays and Onions", a 2 cylinder car with a 5 seater body. Alldays and Onions cars were manufactured in Birmingham by a firm that also made railway engines. Some of the Alldays cars were presented as prizes to purveyors of "Zambuk", a proprietary substance sold in tins, but I cannot remember for what purpose it was used. Anyhow my father acquired this car from someone who had sold so much "Zambuk" that he had received it as a prize. Apparently he had no use for the Alldays, so perhaps he was wise enough to have obtained a car of a better known make.

The "Alldays and Onions" car was green in colour, it had brass oil side lamps and a single acetylene headlamp supplied with acetylene generated by the action of water on calcium carbide in a brass contraption on one of the running boards. Needless to say the illumination provided was totally inadequate for driving after dark, but the consequent hazards were a constant source of merriment to my brother and myself when travelling in the back seat. The car had a bulb horn connected to the bulb by a long, flexible tube. The hand brake and gear lever were situated outside the body of the car and the driver had to pull himself forward on the seat whenever the hand brake or gear lever had to be operated. There was no foot accelerator and a small lever above the steering wheel controlled the carburettor. The ignition was advanced or retarded by a second lever in the same position. Seeing that the car was a heavy five seater body and a 2 cylinder engine, gear changing was unavoidably very frequent and required great skill. Synchromesh gears were then unknown, and double-declutching was essential when changing from a higher to a lower gear. The gearbox was filled with thick oily grease and in cold weather it was really stiff. It is not surprising that the sound of clashing gear wheels was not infrequent, especially on a cold morning. There was great difficulty in getting into top gear for the first time in the day and we frequently had to make a fresh start in the Village Street after leaving the Vicarage. Not surprisingly new sets of gear wheels were required from time to time.

The petrol tank was under the front seat and the petrol flowed from there to the engine by gravity. There was an emergency hand pump for the petrol on the steering column, but I cannot remember this being used so presumably it was ineffective. The net result was that petrol failed to reach the engine on steep hills and it was then necessary to go into reverse and drive backwards. In case of extreme emergency it was possible to lower a spike from underneath the car which stuck into the road surface and so prevented further movement. Although we sometimes got stuck on hills I do not remember that the spike into the road was ever used. Protection against the weather was provided by a canvas hood, which was very difficult to raise, supplemented by side curtains. In bad weather the hood was kept up permanently and some of the side curtains were always in position.

We had many exciting adventures with the "Alldays" and the fact that it could carry 4 passengers in addition to the driver meant that it was in frequent demand for such purposes as taking parishioners to Salisbury infirmary or to the Eye Hospital at Southampton. There was, of course, no ambulance service in those days.

One notable adventure with the "Alldays" was an occasion when my father drove down Newton lane when the road surface was very slippery. Consequently the car skidded and it came to rest traversely across the narrow lane, which was completely blocked to traffic. Hardly had this happened before another car, travelling towards Whiteparish, arrived on the scene and its progress was completely blocked. The occupant of this car proved to be a non-conformist minister on his way to address an audience at the Wesleyan chapel. In those days when there was so much needless animosity between the Church of England and the non-conformists it was a major calamity for the Vicar of Whiteparish to obstruct the passage of a Wesleyan Minister. I feel sure my father must have dealt with the situation very tactfully, but the event probably caused much merriment in the local pubs.

My father actually continued to run the Alldays until about 1920, long after we left Whiteparish, and its behaviour became increasingly unpredictable as the years went by. It was eventually given in part exchange for a second hand "Swift" which gave almost as much trouble as the Alldays. The dealer who took the over the Alldays afterwards complained bitterly about its performance and I was never quite sure who had the worse of the bargain. On one occasion an attempt to dispose of the Alldays was made by offering it for sale in Wimborne market place on market day. The only offer that was made for it was 5/- from a farmer.

I remember the first motor bus that provided a regular service to Whiteparish. It was a box-like vehicle, painted bright yellow, and, as far as I can remember its wheels had solid tyres. Its starting point was at Wellow in the New Forest and it came via Landford to Whiteparish and on to Salisbury, returning in the reverse direction later in the day. Its official stopping place at Whiteparish was by the Vicarage wall. I only remember travelling in the bus on one occasion. The ventilation was poor and there was a good deal of vibration. The lack of ventilation probably meant that it was something of a germ trap and I was unlucky enough to pick up the influenza infection.

I also remember the first occasion when a motor coach came to Whiteparish. It was chartered to convey a party of parishioners, but I cannot remember to what destination but may well be Bournemouth. The coach, like the bus, was yellow in colour and it started from the churchyard gate opposite the Vicarage. Unlike the bus it was an open vehicle of the type to which we then referred as a "motor toast-rack" because the passengers were seated in transverse rows across the coach.

Early Wiltshire & Dorset bus

(The above was written by Charles Russell Metcalfe, son of the Vicar of Whiteparish between 1902 and 1915. Charles Russell Metcalfe, botanist, was born in Whiteparish 11th September 1904. He was appointed Keeper Jodrell Laboratory Royal Botanic Gardens Kew and held that position from 1930 to 1969; he received an OBE in 1966. He died 16th June 1991).

Contrary to what is said above, two of our oldest residents maintain that Mr Gay of Alderstone Farm owned the first car in Whiteparish. It was, they say, a 'Swift' an open car. Mr Gay was a Chapel man and since Mr Metcalfe's memories are based on the cars he saw bringing people to the church the matter is still, as yet, unresolved.

CHAPTER 12

AN UNUSUAL INCIDENT

C. R. Metcalfe's report of an exceptional day
21st September 1912

Special Occasions - Another much more trivial event, which was nevertheless a major sensation at the time when it took place, was an occasion when a large, very ancient elm tree which stood beside the stile leading into the field next to the vicarage was found to be on fire. No doubt the fire was started by children who made use of the hollow space at the base of the trunk in which to start it. This happened on Ascension Day, and a lady named Miss Bristow, who attended the 8 am service was so upset when she heard about the tree that she called the fire brigade from Romsey to extinguish it. I remember the event particularly well because I had never previously seen a fire engine, and the one from Romsey was, at the time a very modern one which was propelled by an internal combustion engine instead being drawn by horses. It was installed in a field on the opposite side of the road from the elm tree. Here there was a pond from which water was pumped on to the burning tree, which was quickly extinguished.

These two photo's must be copies of those mentioned in the text as having been lost

The event was a major talking point in the village for some time afterwards. Photographs of the fire engine were taken from which post cards were made and sold in the village. For many years I had a set of these photographs, but sadly they have been lost. However, the day on which the fire engine came was made even more memorable for the children by a Sunday School outing in the grounds of Miss Bristow's house. So she was a popular figure that day.

(The 'Memories of Whiteparish' by Charles Russell Metcalfe covered the period 1904 - 1915. Mr Metcalfe was the son of Charles Frederick Metcalfe who was the Vicar of Whiteparish at the time.)

CHAPTER 13

WHITEPARISH SCHOOL

An early view of the school

Whiteparish is fortunate to have a thriving primary school. The school was built in 1842 and registered that year on 13th May 1842. The original building consisted of the hall and what is now class 2. Later a porch was built over the entrance and at the end of the 19th century class 3 was added. By 1960 the entire flat roofed area had been added and in 1970 the office space was built.

At a meeting of the Trustees of the Girl's School on 2nd November 1842 it was resolved that the Mistress of the Free School (Girl's School) be allowed to teach in the new schools erected on the Common (Common Road). At the same date Lynch's school, a boy's school was transferred to the new buildings. It seems that although there are references to Boy's School and Girl's School these are in fact both part of the new building.

The school was built to accommodate 160 boys but it seems that from the beginning the two classrooms were a boy's school and a girl's school respectively. The first headmaster was Mr Hayter while Miss Cook was responsible for the girls apparently irrespective of ages. They were both retired in 1859 on a pension of £10 and £5 per annum respectively presumably on the grounds that they were not certificated (academically qualified). A Mr Carter took over for one year and in 1860 two certificated teachers were appointed a Mr Williams as headmaster and a Miss Bell in charge of the girls. It was in this year that the school became a National School under Government inspection.

School photos 1895, school master Mr Faulkner, school mistress Miss Rose Lockyer, many of these children would still have been at school in the1900s.

In 1890 a new Boy's School was erected, in fact a new classroom was added which is now class two in the present building. The old Boy's school, a classroom, was handed over to the Girl's School and the Girl's School became the Infant's School. The Schools were managed by a Management Committee consisting at that time of Earl Nelson, Mr (Squire) Lawrence, Mr Matcham, Capt. Fort, Mr Woodford, Mr Fort, Mr Drake and Mrs (?) Pattison.

In 1895 Mr William's died and the vacancy of Head Master was advertised to which there were 120 applications. The 120 were reduced to 12 who were interviewed and the post was offered to Mr Faulkner at a salary of £100 and a house. In 1897 the school became a mixed school with Mr Faulkner as Headmaster and the references to Girl's School and Boy's School disappeared. At that time there were 46 boys, 46 girls and 35 infants a total of 127 children. Mr Faulkner proved to be a good choice as he filled the post for 35years and had a great influence on the development of the village.

In 1907 there were three teachers under Mr Faulkner and there were 146 children between the ages of five and fourteen on the roll. Unfortunately there was rarely full attendance. The roads in the area must have been very bad because whenever there was heavy rain or snow the attendance was drastically reduced. When this happened no registers were taken. A summary of the weather conditions and absenteeism shows that the weather was bad in the winters from 1913 to 1919 with snow in 1914,1916,1917 and 1918. During the last two of these years the attendances dropped to 15 and 20. After 1919 the weather and roads seem to have been better and attendances were not seriously affected by bad conditions until 1947, when on one day there were two children present in the morning and none in the afternoon. Snow again affected numbers in the winters of 1950, 1954, 1959 and 1965.

There were very few years in which there was no mention of infectious or contagious diseases, although the numbers of children affected are not given except when there was an epidemic. In 1918 influenza closed the school for thirteen days, while in 1923 ten days were lost because of measles. The first inoculations against diphtheria were recorded in 1951 but in 1957 eighty-eight children out of one hundred and thirteen suffered from 'Asian Flu'. Measles again broke out in 1959 when two thirds of the children were affected. There is no note of polio but anti-polio injections were introduced in 1956. There is no note of the severity of the infections for the most part but two children died of scarlet fever, one in 1908 and one in 1911. Two other deaths occurred in 1914 and 1916 but the causes are not stated.

From 1913, at least, there were quite substantial prizes for good attendance, paid by a Trust. Prizes for 90% attendance were as follows: -

Year	Boys and Girls	First	Second
10		£1	10 shillings
11		£2	10 shillings
12		£2 10/-	£1

These were paid when the children left school and entered a trade (apprenticeship?) or occupation. In spite of difficulties with weather and illness over the years, some children did have full attendance. In March 1910 five children had 100% attendance, and in May of the same year silver watches were presented to Nelly Light for 11 years of unbroken and punctual attendance and Dorothy Collins for 9 years of unbroken attendance.

Disease and weather were not the only reasons for school closure. Some sound very pleasant, among them harvest holidays, Sunday school outings, Chrysanthemum Society shows (1907 - 1910), Fete days, blackberry picking, potato weeks and the occasional days when the school was used as a Polling station. In 1917, 162 soldiers of H.A.M.T. were billeted in the school as apparently frost had broken up the roads. There was a holiday in 1920 when Miss H. Faulkner gained a science degree at Bristol University, which is not surprising, since she was the headmaster's daughter. The outbreak of war in 1939 delayed the opening of the school and army manoeuvres closed it for a fortnight in 1951.

Throughout its life the school has been subject to heating problems. There are frequent references to low temperatures, even after the system was renewed in 1909. This was so in the mid-twenties and new heating was installed in 1929. However there was still trouble in the 1930s. The heating failed in 1932 and when it was again faulty in 1933, coal fires were installed in the classrooms. Conditions seem to have been very bad in 1945 and the school was closed in 1948 because fuel gasses leaked into the classrooms from a faulty boiler. Finally, in 1952, a newly installed heating system was "thought to be efficient".

The first mention in these reports of difficulties with the lavatories was in 1927 when the caretaker complained and the Medical Officer of Health was called in. In 1932 the school was inspected with a view to improving the water supply. Although the reports do not say so specifically, the water for the school at that time seems to have come from wells in the grounds and in 1939 the decision was made to boil all drinking water drawn from these wells.

In 1955 builders were asked to assess the rebuilding of the school and there was talk of the possibilities of water closets. In 1957 there was again talk of new sewerage and drainage systems. Plans for new toilets and classrooms were made in September and December but there is no further mention of these plans. On June 23rd 1960 a violent storm flooded the pump. Because there was no sanitation the school was closed and a new pump was put in. (The Headmaster's records are not accessible after 1968, so further information comes from Governors' reports). There is no record of trouble with sewerage until 1970, when again the septic tank caused problems. At last, in 1971, the school was connected to the main drains.

The Headmaster's reports do not give much information about the syllabus followed by the school. The 'basic' subjects are never mentioned but academic successes are sometimes recorded. The first mention of the County Examinations (1930) noted that 11 pupils sat; 8 passed and 3 failed. 4 pupils (1 girl and 3 boys) gained places at Bishops School between 1921 and 1923. Another boy entered Bishops in 1933 and a girl went on to the County Secondary School in 1935. In 1942, 4 pupils gained scholarships.

Music is rarely mentioned until the late fifties. School concerts were held in 1955 and 1957. In 1970 Mrs East had a recorder consort under tuition and by Jan 1971 she was teaching 28 pupils to play. This number rose to 36 by September of that year. Percussion was added and new percussion and tuned pitch instruments were obtained in 1972.

Sports were also important and there are frequent references to football matches against other schools and in 1951 George Curtis (a footballer from Southampton) came to the school to give a talk and coaching. In 1952 cricket and netball were also played. From 1933 the Area Sports was a regular event.

Whiteparish school team taking part in the area sports day in Downton year unknown

The care of the school gardens was obviously a most important part of the syllabus. It was first mentioned, in the records we have seen, in 1911, when it was 'inspected' and from then on its progress was followed. Fruit trees were planted (1918), seeds and plants bought and the effect of the weather on its cultivation was monitored. In 1942, during the 2nd World War, the South Wiltshire Grammar School canteen was supplied with produce from the garden. Even the disasters were noted. In 1928 "the school gardens were ruined by Mr Page's cows". In 1938, forest ponies got into the garden and further damage resulted in a visit from the Agister. Twelve years later they broke in again. The change in the organisation of the school in 1955, mainly the loss of the senior pupils, made a great difference to the gardens and that year it was decided to grass them over. However, in 1957 some of it was still producing strawberries and peas and new trees had been planted.

Another successful venture was the Poultry Club. This was first proposed in January 1935 and its first lesson, on poultry keeping, was in March. The first meeting of the club was in May 1936. The members held shares and hoped eventually to share in any profits. There followed lessons in Trussing and Culling, Moulting and Incubation. The club seems to have done well; in September 1938 they won a first and fourth place in the schools section of a Challenge Competition and in October they won a Silver Challenge Cup. In 1939 an incubator was bought but that was the last reference to the club. In 1939 there was a proposal to start a Pig Club but pig keeping seems to have been started privately by the then Headmaster and extended to the village

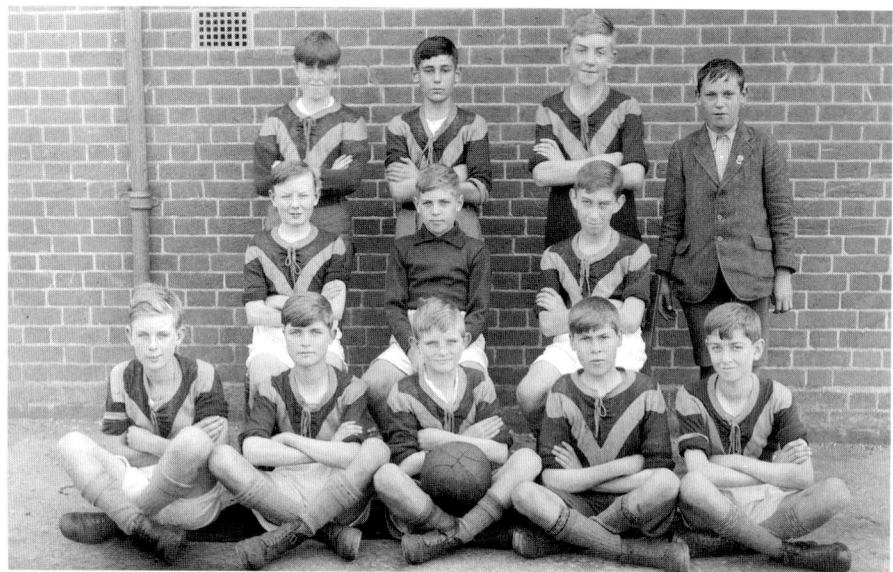

School football team mid 1930s

Senior school photo mid 1930s

Girl's interests were provided for in the syllabus (netball for example) and there were courses in housewifery and cookery (held in the Wesleyan Hall in 1922), Domestic Economy (1927) and the first Domestic Science lesson started in 1929. In 1957 pupils went to Salisbury for woodwork (boys) and Domestic Sciences classes (girls). Sewing was obviously on the timetable because new sewing machines were delivered in 1936.

There are references in later years to new introductions to the school, which must have affected teaching methods. The children were introduced to radio in 1935 and the first schools programmes started in 1936. Electricity was brought in in 1948, the telephone in 1967 and television in 1968. Now they have computers.

Very little is said about the two World Wars. Some Belgian refugee children arrived in November and December 1914, but nothing is mentioned about how long they stayed. Peace celebrations were held in October 1919 having been postponed from July because of bad weather. These included a tea, cinema entertainment and the gift of a mug. The school appears to have been more involved in the 2nd War. There were evacuees in 1939 "in and out" and twelve were present in 1942. As has already been mentioned, the school was used by the troops once or twice (it was prepared as a rest centre in 1942). Scrap was collected, 2 tons 17 cwt of scrap iron and 19cwt of paper. This was sold and the school received 25% of the proceeds, the Forces received 75%. There were a number of remarkable collections of money. In the spring of 1942 a 'Warship Week' collection took in £246 19s 6d and the total raised in the village by the children was £474 16s 6d. A 'Wings for Victory' collection raised £531 10s 0d and a 'Salute to Soldiers' collection in 1944 raised £574 5s 0d. There is no note of any celebrations at the cessation of war and it was not until November 1963 that an Armistice Day ceremony was mentioned.

The headmaster Mr Baker and the senior school pupils 1946

There were some out of school activities besides sports. The first reference to a 'school trip' was on June 7th 1934 when children were taken to the Royal Counties Show. Later there was an outing to Southampton. In 1936, 26 children and 16 adults went to London and spent a full day visiting the sights, the Houses of Parliament, Buckingham Palace, Regents Park Zoo and St. Paul's Cathedral. There were no trips during the war but children went to Weymouth in 1951 and to Bournemouth in 1952. 26 senior and intermediate children went on a camping holiday in 1953. Sandbanks and Bournemouth were visited in 1956, Swanage in 1957 and London Airport in 1958. Subsequently there were visits to other places in the area usually to the seaside.

Dr Peter Claydon being 'gunked' during a school fete'

The full school records for the past 30 years are not available to researchers, but the following paragraphs have been gleaned from the published Governor's reports. It is worth saying that the Manager's Committee of earlier years was replaced by a Board of Governors on 5th May 1980. A School Association raised funds with Fetes and

Jumble Sales etc. until it was disbanded in 1992 when a Parent Teachers' Association (P.T.A.) was set up. The School has been decorated at intervals, sometimes rather too long intervals, dependant on school funds. At one time in the late 1980s or early 1990s a group of parents set to and decorated the infant's class during one holiday. The Library was built and heated with funds contributed by the P.T.A. following a very successful 'Auction of Promises' that raised £3000 and a Fete during which there was an hilarious 'Gunking' session that raised £1000

The school has most years since 1979 had outings to various sites, Windsor, Brownsea Island, Bournemouth etc. with the Infants going on a less strenuous trip and the juniors a more adventurous one.

Music and Song has featured as an extra curricula activity for many years, and pantomimes, put on by the children, have proved very popular and increasingly 'professional'. A trip to Salisbury Playhouse Pantomime has been 'a last day before Christmas Holidays' treat for several years. Cycling Proficiency Practice and Testing has been a popular extra, too, it was first proposed in 1977. Computers were first mentioned in 1981 and now each class has its own computer and software

School showing the new library in the centre 1999

Comprehensive Schooling was being discussed in 1979 and no enthusiasm amongst the staff was shown when it was planned to move 9 year olds to Downton sometime after that, it was felt that the long day would be too much for the young ones to cope with. The first entry regarding the National Curriculum was in 1989. There have been a steady number of children going into the Grammar Schools over the past 30 years.

Safety for the children around the school has been a priority to Staff and Governors, in 1978 they were pressing for yellow markings to be painted outside the school, to restrict parking. There was even a survey of traffic but it was not until 1997 that the road was marked. Also the school field has been fenced but only on three sides of the field.

In common with all primary schools, milk was no longer distributed in 1980 and in the same year it was announced that the school dinner was not, any longer, to be assumed to be the child's main meal. In 1983 the senior citizens of the village were invited to join the children at lunch once a month, which proved very popular with both age groups.

The school has seldom had to close over recent years only two occasions being recorded and each time because of an exceptional snowfall. On the whole the children have been well avoiding all the epidemics of the earlier part of the century. The only mention of childish illness was a report of four children having whooping cough in 1989.

Regular games of netball and football are played against other primary schools in the area and Sports Days are held each year, recently they have been rounded off with a B.B.Q.

At Government's request alarms and safety lights have been installed, and hopefully the occasional 'break-ins' of 1982,1987 and 1989, are a thing of the past.

Photograph of the whole school celebrating the 150th anniversary of the founding of the school in 1992. Head teacher Mr Truman and other teachers, governors, assistants and children in Victorian costume

CHAPTER 14

A LETTER FROM A BOY OF 14 YEARS OF AGE AROUND 1917.

I was at school until I was 13 years old. Then I left, if it had not been for the War I would have had to stay until I was 14. Mother found me a job, and because there were so few men about to do work on the farms, the school said and the Government said, I could leave.

I help Mr. Collins the cobbler who lives in the Street. He keeps half a dozen cows and I help him look after them. Once I got the hang of milking these cows he leaves me to get on with the job. It means starting work at 7 o'clock in the morning, milk and feed the animals, clean out their sheds and then if it is summer time help with the hay making or mangel hoeing, until it is time to milk in the afternoon. During the summer I have to work after teatime if crops have to be gathered. Sundays we only milk and feed the cows.

Sometimes I have to drive the cows from pasture the other side of the main road and if it has been wet the Dove lane is a foot deep in water. To save my feet getting wet I jump on the back of the friendly old cow and she will carry me through the water. Mr Collins pays me five shillings a week and some milk. Mother takes most of my wages for my keep.

When there is no work to be done me and my mates from school or work take our 'cattypolts' down to the Common and hunt squirrels or anything we can find. Sometimes we make a cricket bat and stumps and someone gave us an old ball, and we play on the Common in front of the school. Sometimes we have to drive the cattle away before we can play.

CHAPTER 15

NOTES FROM A PRIMARY
SCHOOL BOY 1999

There are lots of sports and things to do in Whiteparish. At school we play football, netball, rounders and in the summer we go swimming. We have optional after school clubs, dance, first aid, and Judo that takes place at lunchtime. As well as the normal subjects we do in class, I also have to fix the class's computers as they keep going wrong!

Outside school I go to football training at the 'Rec' on Wednesday. I also go to the sports club where we play football, pool, table football, table tennis, snooker and darts.

There is a children's play area at the 'Rec' as well as the sports club. Among other things I do in my spare time are going on bike rides, playing in the Bramleys, but my favourite pastime of all is playing on my P.C. (personal computer). I do that a lot (understatement of the millennium) and that is just some of the things I do in 1999.

Steven Burr.

CHAPTER 16

MY TEENAGE LIFE IN WHITEPARISH IN 1999

As a 14-year-old boy living in Whiteparish in the County of Wiltshire, I am glad to live away from the crowded cities. Big cities are usually dirty, polluted and cramped and there is lots of traffic, but Whiteparish, eight miles from the nearest town, Salisbury, is a clean, beautiful and quiet village.

However the problem I have with Whiteparish is to do with occupying myself. Being a small village means there is little in the way of things to do, although there is a sports club on Wednesday evenings. During the dark winter months we can play games such as table tennis, snooker, pool, and darts and when we get to the summer months we can also play football, tennis, rounders and other outdoor sports. The club has also started to organise days out, when we can go to watch or play sports that we would not have had much chance to do normally. We have already been to see a basketball match between Salisbury and the Isle of Wight, which was very enjoyable, even though Salisbury, who I was supporting, lost by four points.

Also on Wednesdays, I have to deliver the 'Avon Advertiser' newspaper to all the houses in Common Road, Clay Street and Hop Gardens. It takes me over an hour and a half and I don't get paid much but some money is better than none. When it is warm and sunny, delivering the paper is quite a pleasurable job but during the winter when it is very cold I wish I didn't have the job at all.

Sometimes I go to one of my friends' houses or he comes round to my house or we go to the Recreation ground to play football or basketball. If no one is in then I either stay in or go into Salisbury to the snooker club or to just walk around.

During school days I get home at about four o'clock and then I usually stay in to do my homework or revision for any exams I may have to take.

Sometimes I wonder how Whiteparish will look in a hundred years time, whether it will be built up and much larger than it is now or whether it may not even be here then. For all I know everybody could have moved into the cities to find better work or bigger houses. I hope that doesn't happen otherwise a very beautiful little village will be lost for ever.

Anthony Munro

CHAPTER 17

WHITEPARISH - AN ACTIVE VILLAGE.

The village of Whiteparish has, throughout the century had many and various activities and clubs. We are fortunate that the village has a village hall, a Methodists hall, a Youth Club, a Cricket Pavilion and the 'King's Head' Meeting Room for the use of the modern clubs.

Members of the Youth Club setting out on a trip to Paris

In the early years of the century the 'Lynches' was used as a Reading Room and Boys Club. In 1902 a Mr Hayter made a gift of books to the Parochial Lending Library and by 1907 the Reading Room was re-established, having gone through a bad patch. A comment was made by the editor of the day in the 'Whiteparish & Landford Parish Magazine that "such a club is sorely needed in the village as there is a great deal too much loafing about and bad language in 'the street' at night". We now have the Mobile Library visiting the village every other week. The Boys Club fell out of favour and the enthusiastic Mr Doel and a group of young teenagers revived a Youth Club when they were offered the use of a stable block in the grounds of Abbotstone House in 1958. The group of 4 boys and 5 girls earned the money necessary to equip the stable block by cleaning out a broiler house that had held 16000 chickens, a job which took five evenings work. Later in 1959 they spent many evenings stripping down an Air Hanger at Stoney Cross which had been used by the Air Force during World War 2, to earn more money for the Club. Work on the stable block consisted of taking out a cobbled floor and laying a new concrete one, taking out iron hay boxes, replacing rotten boards and painting and equipping the room with a stage, refreshment bar, easy chairs, T V, radio and stove - many items being donated by villagers in November 1958. A formal opening ceremony was held with parents and supporters being amazed by the work done and effect achieved by the young group. The Youth Club was very active attending Speedway Racing, repairing and eventually sailing a yacht in Southampton Water, making a trip to Paris, performing Pantomimes etc.

The original group of youngsters either married or moved out of the village and unfortunately the youngsters replacing them were less dedicated and once again the club drifted into oblivion. Due mainly to the efforts of Peter Bunce and supported by numerous parents and young people of the village, the Youth Club was restarted in 1981, with early meetings held in the cricket pavilion. Support and help from well-wishers of the community, various grants and members efforts made it possible for the new club to obtain its own building which was erected next to the pavilion in 1983. Construction and fitting out of the club by volunteers and members took another two years. From then on the youngsters of the village had the use of Snooker, Pool, Darts, Music, Tuck Shop and other activities. Membership during this period varied from as many as 35 to as few as 3, but none failed to enjoy themselves and in their own particular way, contributed to its success. A junior club also ran for a short time later. The Club closed in 1995 and great efforts went into repairing and decorating the building. A few parents of young teenagers then proposed a Sports Club to be run by parents, with children, with as often as possible parents joining in the games. There is now a thriving Sports Club playing Football, Tennis, Rounders, Darts, Pool and any other team game that can be organised. There is also a very popular 'Tuck Shop' and a youth football team "Team Elite" playing matches at weekends and practising on Sports Club evenings.

The Badminton Club is another active club, which was first started when a National player, Betty Bond, moved into the village and began to teach the game to interested villagers. In no time at all a Club was formed to meet at the village hall on Monday evenings. This meeting became over subscribed and a second evening's play now takes place on Tuesday. There was a thriving youth section trained by Jean James from 1971 to 1993. Badminton had been played at the youth club for some years before 1970 under the supervision of David Crombie and has continued sporadically up to 1993.

The Cubs have had regular meetings since well before 1962 and the stalwarts Ann and Bob Meehan who took over the group in 1984 now run the group. The boys go Camping each year and have active weekly meetings. The numbers are small but they are an enthusiastic group.

Cub scouts in carnival mood - mid 1990s, Ann and Bob Meeham keeping order

The tiny children are well served by the Teddy Bear Club meeting once a week in the village hall on Friday at 10am. The Club is a social contact for mothers with young children who are too young to join the 'Pre-school Group'. The mothers pay £1 a meeting and enjoy a cup of tea or coffee, a biscuit and a chat, while the children play with a variety of toys and have their refreshments. There are currently 20 children on the register.

Pepperbox pre-school group 1999

The children who are able to be left on their own without their mothers are able to join the Pre-school Group, otherwise known as the Pepperbox Pre-school play group, which meets four mornings a week Mondays to Thursdays. It was started way back in 1968 and has had its ups and downs but is thriving at present. It has a paid-trained leader and a committee of mums. With modern legislation there are many more legal restrictions put upon such groups, employment law and minimum pay have to be honoured. The playgroup also has an Ofsted inspection regularly and the committee is quite confident that the report due out soon, following the June inspection, will be a good one. At around four and a half years of age the children move on to the reception class at the school.

On Sundays the Sunday school has a small membership under the guidance of several young mums. The Church choir is thriving and has done for many years. There is mention in the Church magazine of 1907 of an outing to Bournemouth enjoyed by some members of the choir although many had to be left in the village to help with the harvest. In the 1970's Rev Keeley and his wife Pat stimulated the interests of many youngsters in music, training a steady flow of singers. Previous choir members have shown particular musical talent, singing in Salisbury Cathedral choir, joining a professional opera group, singing as a choir member in St. Pauls Cathedral and a few joining together to form "Sarum Impromptu" performing concerts for charitable causes. Mrs Keeley for many years after her husband's death trained the choir eventually handing over to Annette Todd. When Dr. David Tyrrell assumed the position of Organist after the long service of more than 50 years of Mrs Hayes and later Pat Keeley he has assisted Annette Todd with the choir training. Pat Keeley has since 1983 trained the 'mini songsters' very young children those too young to join the church choir. It is worth mentioning that she has trained these little ones to a very high standard entering them in the Salisbury young peoples festival of music, even encouraging a few to perform solo items. Annette Todd and Dr Tyrrell currently take the choir to Festivals of choir music at various venues in the Diocese, have regular trips to Pantomimes and musical shows and have a 'Sailing Day' near Christchurch. They also go carol singing around the village at Christmas

The game of cricket has been played in Wiltshire all this century. The results of cricket matches played by a Whiteparish team against other village teams is reported in several village and church magazines of the early 1900's. Mr Faulkner, the schoolmaster, and other village men at that time were known to have walked to West Tytherley for some Saturday matches. The team has been entertaining a side from Sheffield for 44 years. This came about when a Dr Harding came from Sheffield to live in Abbotstone House and took up a post at Salisbury Infirmary in the Pathology department in 1956. At that time the team from Sheffield was made up with his students and ex-students, but later included members of Hallamshire Cricket Club whose captain was a Dr Cox. Dr Harding used to entertain both teams to dinner after the game, which from all accounts was a great evening. It was rumoured that the good doctor recommended drinking best bitter beer as it flushed out the bacteria from the kidneys! The sons of both teams still meet when Sheffield come to tour, but the older members now play an occasional game of golf. The team from Sheffield has, over the years, made many friends in the parish and it is to be hoped that this arrangement will continue well into the next century. The current team is riding high in their league. A highlight of recent years was when the England Women's Cricket team, captained by Sue Metcalfe the sister of one of the Whiteparish team, played a 45 over match against the Whiteparish team in April of 1992 ostensibly to raise funds for the Ladies World Cup Squad and the Whiteparish junior cricket teams. The visitors won by 22 runs.

SOUVENIR PROGRAMME
No: 280

CRICKET

SPONSORED
EXHIBITION MATCH

WHITEPARISH C.C.
VERSUS
AN ENGLAND LADIES XI

AT

THE MEMORIAL
RECREATION GROUND
WHITEPARISH
SATURDAY 25 APRIL 1992
START 2pm

Lucky Number Programme Draw

Programme cover of England Ladies eleven 1992

Whiteparish Football Team 1962

Association football is also played regularly in the village but details of the earlier years are not recorded in the magazines we have read. As often happens, the fortunes of football teams wax and wane and the Whiteparish Club team has been no exception. The war years interrupted play and it was not until 1962 that Mr Ben McCrow, Mr Ken Feltham and the landlord of the White Hart, Mr Tom Fenwick succeeded in getting a team together and entered the 5th division of a local league. Within three years they had reached division 2. Having a pitch on the Memorial Ground helped a great deal, as prior to this ground being available, games were played on a lower meadow along Newton Lane, which was often flooded.

Whiteparish Football Team 1999

↝↜ Programme ↝↜

(1)	**THE DEAR DEPARTED**
	A Comedy in One Act
	by
	Stanley Houghton

CAST

Mrs. Slater...	...	...	...	...	Elsie Chandler
Mrs. Jordan	...	...	...	...	Jean Dear
Henry Slater	...	...	...	...	John Tubb
Ben Jordan	...	...	...	...	Thomas Fenwick
Victoria Slater	...	...	...		Jacqueline Edmonds
Abel Merryweather	...	...	...		Harold Baker

(2)	**DARK BROWN**
	A Melodrama in One Act
	by
	Philip Johnson

CAST

Mrs. Collins	...	...	...	...	Lily Tucker
Miss Tasker	...	...	...	...	Bridget Peters
Jenny Brown	...	...	...	...	Lilian Edmonds
Bella Crewe	...	...	...	...	Margaret Baker
Fred Whitworth	...	...	...		Chris Peters
Mrs Persophelous	...	...	...		Roslyn Stuart
Arthur Brown	...	...	...	...	Thomas Fenwick

(3)	**INTERVAL**
	Refreshments will be served

(4)	**A NOD, SNEEZE, AND A GOAT**
	A Comedy in One Act
	by
	Mabel Constanduros and Howard Agg

CAST

Mrs. Sparkes	...	...	...	...	Rose Pointer
Mr. Sparkes	...	...	...	...	Vernon James
Mrs Boeking	...	...	...	...	Betty Feltham
District Nurse	...	...	...	...	Lady Ransford Slater

(5)	**THE BONNY EARL O' MORAY**
	A Comedy in One Act
	by
	Stuart Ready

CAST

Miss Alice Twiddly	...	...	...		Bridget Peters
Florrie	...	...	...	...	Barbara Beauchamp
Mrs. Hester Lumley	...	...	...		Betty Feltham
Gloria Lumley	...	...	...	...	Eileen Rackham
Mrs. Egham	...	...	...	...	Margaret Baker

Plays Produced by Roslyn Stuart

Stage Manager, Edward Doel

Lighting, Scenery and Recorded Music by
Edward Doel and Thomas Fenwick

Copy of a programme of short plays performed by the Whiteparish Drama Club in 1948

The village has had for most of the years of this century a thriving group of actors. Plays were presented by the Whiteparish Drama Group soon after the end of World War 2 and the Pepperbox Players, their successors, have put on Christmas pantomimes and occasional plays since 1986 and as mentioned in this book elsewhere the Youth Club performed Pantomimes regularly in the 1950's and 1960's

The Pepperbox Players in costume for 'One of our haystacks is missing' July 1988

Members of the Pepperbox Players 1999

Women in the village have many opportunities for social contact. The longest standing Club is the Mother's Union whose Whiteparish branch was set up in 1924. Members meet each month for talks, tea, and chat. The Methodists have a 'Women's Bright Hour' who meet together every other week in the Methodists schoolroom for similar entertainment. Around 30 young mums formed the Women's Institute within the village in September 1946. The current membership is 38 who are decidedly not young mums any longer. They meet monthly for talks, slide shows, chat and the famous W.I. teas. There is in the village just one of the original members, Mrs Iris McPhail, whose memories are quoted elsewhere in this book.

Whiteparish Womens Institute Members, plus speaker, October 1999

The Friendship Club was set up during 1974. Bill Hogg who had just moved into the village was approached by the Rev. Richard Collington to try to set up a Club for retired people and those who were lonely, sick or housebound. Now within the village, those with bigger gardens often open them for garden parties, outings are arranged and are very popular, and picnics were held in the New Forest. Inn addition there have been trips to hear Military Band Concerts and to Devizes to see Craft Exhibitions all with the help of 'Age Concern'. The Club was invited to the Woolworth's Christmas Shopping evening where seasonal fare and drinks were provided and the Salvation Army Band played carols and provided a most enjoyable evening.

Within the Church there is a thriving 'Altar Guild'. The group regularly produces beautiful floral arrangements in the Church all the year round. Particularly they make a special effort during Whiteparish Week making floral arrangements to a chosen theme.

In order to fund repairs to the village hall and to augment running costs the village hall committee are involved in a '100 plus' Club. This was started in 1978 by Ken Wootton and Lionel Moores and is still going strong. The annual subscription of £12 is put to good use providing four cash prizes each month and eight at Christmas. Approximately half of the money raised goes to fund the prizes and the remainder is put into the Hall Fund. The number of members is now approaching 200.

Finance is very much to the fore in the Whiteparish Share Club. This Club was formed in 1995 and now has 20 members only one of whom can be called professional or has worked in financial services. Decisions are made as to which shares to invest in after a meal at local hostelry. We are assured that the fun of eating out and sharing a drink or two helps with the decision making, which in the first year of the Club's being enabled them to win top position in a competition with 500 competing clubs run by 'Proshare' an organisation set up to promote share ownership. The win caused quite a stir in the media, the 'Times' and 'Daily Express', Local and National Radio and T.V. all asked for interviews and photocalls.

Members and friends of the Whiteparish Garden Club attending the 1999 Flower and Hobbies Show

The current Garden Club was formed in 1973 but as we have seen a Schedule of a 'Chrysanthemum Show' being held in the schoolroom on 18th November 1904 and as there is no indication that it was the first we can assume shows were being held before that date. The first Flower Shows were held in Melchet Court and the villagers used to walk across the fields to the show. Later shows were held in Cowesfield House. Later still the school hall was used but as the number of show exhibits grew the village hall was called into use. In 1905 the most valuable prize was 6/-(30 pence) for 12 blooms (not less than 6 varieties) which was a considerable amount of money in those days. By 1939 the top prize was 10/- (50 pence) for a collection of 6 vegetables. During the 1939-45 war Flower and Produce Shows were held in conjunction with the village fete which was organised by the Whiteparish Red Cross Working Party. Money raised was put to Red Cross Funds. During the early 1970s the Whiteparish Horticultural Club was formed and at a later date this name was changed to the Whiteparish Garden Club. This club has held regular meetings throughout the years and also an annual Flower and Hobbies Show, usually during the month of August, which is one of the highlights of the village year.

Another annual event held within the village is the Whiteparish Week, usually towards the end of May or the beginning of June. During the week many villages are drawn together to join in a quiz, a car treasure hunt, a tug-o-war competition, a car boot sale, and children's races etc. culminating in a Fete on the Saturday. The whole Week is organised by the Stewardship Committee.

Doctor Peter Claydon and friends taking part in the parade during a Carnival Week

Villagers having fun during the Carnival, P.C John Barrow and his wife Margaret in fancy dress.

Probably the largest outdoor event to take place around Whiteparish is the Salisbury and South Wiltshire Agricultural Show. It has been held on the 'Show Ground' at Tower Farm for eight years. Originally it was held in Salisbury, but it became too expensive and difficult to organise there so the venue was changed to a farm site. It was felt that the Salisbury district should continue to have a show, as this area is still predominantly agricultural. The Show has purposely been kept as traditional as possible, whilst demonstrating modern methods and ideas. This can be seen in the farm livestock classes with old favourites such as cattle and sheep alongside llamas and alpacas, where usually the exhibits are of a high standard. The class for the best hay is keenly contested by local farmers and the handspun fibre competition produces some superb work, again, mostly local. There is a variety of trade stands and stands demonstrating the rural crafts of thatching, stick dressing, woodcarving, spinning etc. The bee keeping display is popular as is the band playing in the natural amphitheatre of an old chalk pit. Heavy horses feature largely and the parade of these animals in shining, clinking harness is worth watching. A comprehensive show of horses of all kinds is held, together with a more modern innovation, a donkey show, which has become more popular every year. An 'exemption dog show' caters for family pets from a wide area. Contrasting with the 'state of the art' tractors displayed on the trade stands, vintage tractors and machinery are able to work, ploughing and grass cutting as in days gone by, providing a great attraction for many who congregate round them. The drive past of these machines in the main ring is a fine sight. Those who visit the Show regularly say that they like the quiet, friendly, nostalgic atmosphere and the chance to catch up on trends in agriculture and countryside activities

The tractor display at the show 1999

There is a 'Carers' support group who meets monthly at the doctor's surgery. There is also a 'Link' scheme organised to give aid of almost any sort to people in genuine need from hospital visits, changing library books, taking pets to the vet to taking non drivers to essential appointments.

The heavy horses at the Salisbury and South Wiltshire Agricultural Show 1997

In 1998 the childrens' play area in the Memorial Ground was brought up to date by putting a new safety surface under the swings slides etc. At the same time the large old climbing frame was removed and replaced with a 'state of the art' slide and other more modern play equipment. The money to meet the cost of this update was raised by a hard working group of women within the village.

The Whiteparish History and Environmental Association is the latest group to be formed. Talks are arranged at least 3 times a year on almost any subject relating to local or national history or to the environment. A sub committee has spent two years amassing information and photographs in preparation for this book.

The only picture we have of the Rifle Club taken in the Chalk Pit

During the first half of the century there were many more clubs and groups in the village, but as they closed down no records were kept and therefore few details are known about them. There was a 'Rifle Club', which met on the site where the village hall now stands. There was also a 'Cadet Force' for the young men of the village. For quite a few years there was an annual gymkhana. There was a 'Rat and Sparrow' club formed with cash payments of 3d a dozen for grown sparrows, 2d a dozen for unfledged birds and 1d each for rats tails. This club was formed, no doubt, because both rats and sparrows were considered pests by the farming communities. There was also a village 'Brass Band' that was in great demand at festivities and celebrations. Mr Lockyer was Bandmaster for many years.

Early picture of the village brass band

CHAPTER 18

CELEBRATIONS OF CORONATIONS AND JUBILEES

1900 - 2000

Edward 7th - 1902

The Parish Council had to postpone the celebrations of Edward 7th's Coronation because he had to undergo an operation for appendicitis. We cannot find any reference in the minutes to indicate if any fun and games took place later. However the Church magazine of this period does recall events which can be read under Church history. It does seem that the tent Committee which was given the task of constructing a massive tent for Edward's celebrations was also called upon to do the same for George the 5th's Coronation nine years later.

George 5th - 1911

The Coronation of George 5th took place on Thursday June 22nd 1911. It would seem from the minutes of the council that the whole parish took the day off! At 11a.m. The Rev. Metcalfe, helped by the Nonconformist leader Mr Lampard who read the lesson, held a service in the Church. The village band helped with the music at the service. Then lead by the vicar, followed by the Churchwardens, Parish Councillors, Nobility of the parish, Friendly Societies with banners flying, then village folk and following all these people the village band took up the rear and played the procession to the school. A large Union Jack was unfurled by the Parson (this flag was provided by a worthy member of the parish) and three cheers for the King were called for.

All then went to Parsonage meadow for the 'real meat' of the day. First of all, Dinner (meaning lunch in today's language) was taken in a large tent. This tent was made by joining together farmers rick tarpaulins, a special committee was formed to see to this task, and a task it must have been for the tent was 156 feet long by 24 feet wide! Three lines of tables and seats provided room for 600 people! It must have been a tight squeeze. Squire Lawrence and Lord Nelson made speeches, and it would seem others, and finally a loyal toast was drunk. Lord Nelson provided a hundred medals to commemorate the occasion and these were given to 100 school children. (are any of these still about ?)

The ladies of the village, as far as we can find out, cooked the dinner, how or upon what it is difficult to imagine. One person remembers his mother telling him about this event and in particular her serving a very old lady. This old lady must have been a character who when asked if she would like some more potatoes said "Cor lummy no Mrs., no more taties, but I'll have some more meat, for meat to me is like corn to an 'oss'" (For those who are not up in horse feeding, a diet of corn make them very frisky). Meat did not often occur in a farm worker's diet, so one can see what joy it was for this old lady!

Coronation tent, Whiteparish 26th June 1911

Rain spoilt the organised sports program that afternoon, so it was finished on the next day. Food left over from the first day was given on the Friday to all children under 15 years of age. After 5 p.m. dancing took place in the tent until 10 p.m., music by the village band, but on the second evening, the parish had to call on a portion of the Woodfalls band and had to pay them 30 shillings. One wonders if the village band over indulged the day before or did they have to work that second day! During the evening a cricket match was played between the ladies and gentlemen. The gentlemen had to bat with just broomsticks held in the left hand. The match was drawn at 27 runs each.

The cost of the activities came to £77. It seems that £84 was collected from the villagers the balance being given to the Salisbury Infirmary.

Breakdown of expenditure: -

Sports prizes	£11. 6s. 0d
Meat	£21. 0s. 0d
Baker	£16. 0s. 0d
Mineral drinks	£4. 0s. 0d
Beer	£6. 6s. 0d
Band	£6. 0s. 0d
Other costs (?)	£12. 0s. 0d

George 6th - 1936

Collection by public subscription raised £93.

Little is recorded about the actual day, but 10 lbs of grease was purchased for the grease pole event.

Expenditure
120 mugs for children	£ 6. 5s. 0d.
Sports prizes	£25. 0s. 0d.
Sundries	£22. 0s. 0d.
Catering	£33. 19s. 0d.
	£87. 4s. 0d.

What happened to the balance is not recorded.

It is perhaps interesting to note that over the period 1911 to 1935 the amount of money collected was similar. It had risen quite a lot by 1937. Did this mean that the wealth of the village was beginning to improve, or was it at last coming out of the depression of the 1930's ?

Queen Elizabeth 2nd - 1953

1953 celebrations, parade walking up 'The Street'

As far as we can find out the Parish Council gave encouragement to a committee who organised the event. A house to house collection raised £168, in addition £10. 16s. was obtained from profit from a dance, the British Legion gave £5. 5s. and two worthies of the village gave £5 each. Total collected £205. 1s. 7d.

Expenditure	Firex Co. fireworks	£23. 2s.
	Ham	£31. 10s.
	Edward's shop. Sweets	£18. 13s.
	Sports prizes	£37. 0s
	Music	£5. 0s.

It seems that the total expenditure amounted to £187. 10s. that does not equate with the list of costs. However the balance over was £17. 10s. 8d. which was split between the village hall and the Memorial Ground Charity.

We have heard from one source that at the dinner in the hall, as the guests were waiting for grace to be said, while standing at the tables, a bird's nest fell from the central tower and landed in a plate of food. Much laughter!

Playgroup float 1977 Carnival

Some of the women of the village celebrating Prince Charles marriage to Princess Diana 1981

CHAPTER 19

WHITEPARISH AT WAR

First World War, 1914-1918

We have not been able to find a great deal about this period in the life of the Parish. We have been able to find sermons justifying the war, if not preached within the parish, certainly printed in full, having been delivered from Church headquarters in Salisbury.

There is a reference to a meeting called in the early months of the war by the National Patriotic League. At this meeting people were asked to help Belgian refugees, to form a ladies committee to collect clothes and give physical help, should it be needed, if wounded soldiers should come to convalesce in the village.

Many men in the district had joined the Wiltshire Yeomanry. The idea was that these men, many connected to the countryside, could keep a riding horse or hunter which the government would subsidise, so that if war came the army had cavalry ready to call on at a moment's notice. One reference to this comes from an old resident of the village, whose father had been 'called up' having been a member of the Yeomanry.

After the early defeats in France and the tremendous loss of workhorses used in their thousands to move guns and stores, the parish horse population began to be raided by the War Office. We have accounts of this happening. Rowdens Farm had several of their best plough team carthorses taken and even, in one instance, one or two animals were taken when working on the road. The carts were just left, horse and harness enlisted for France; this is a recorded incident which took place in a small lay-by near Newton Lane. At this stage in the war enemy submarines had not done enough to disrupt food supply, but when a crisis came in 1917, a scramble was on to find the necessary horses for the farms, so that more ground could be ploughed for food production. We have come across accounts of mules from Argentina and the USA coming to the rescue.

As the road, the present A 27, was then the main route from Salisbury Plain to the Southampton Docks it was from all accounts very busy. There was certainly a problem in the summer, when all this traffic caused so much dust, for the road did not have a hard surface. In one winter during the war, the weather was very frosty and the chalk road over Pepperbox Hill, having very little foundation, heaved into a mass of slippery mud such that troops and transports had to come over in small groups forcing units to wait, perhaps over night, for others to catch up. This often meant staying in Whiteparish.

The Parish Council, in 1917, asked the County Council if they would put a hard surface on the road, but to no avail as the County was stretched just with keeping up with requests from the War Office for new and improved roads on the Salisbury Plain.

The only other reference from the Parish minutes regarding the war effort is a demand from the local war agricultural committee that the allotments, around what is now the village hall, should be cultivated. This request was made in early 1918, but it seemed that manpower was not available to do the work. This is reflected in Mr Jack Woodford's memories recorded elsewhere in this book. He tells how he obtained permission to leave school at 13 years of age, as he was needed on the farm. He helped Mr Collins with his six cows and for this work he got six shillings a week. Mr Collins had a smallholding where Upper Young's Farm bungalow now stands. The foundations of the byres still show in the grass.

The shooting season was extended beyond February 1st, so that more birds could be shot for the pot! We have references elsewhere in this book that soldiers came to this Parish from the Remount Camp at Romsey to act as beaters for the pheasant shoots. It would seem, from our interviews with older folk in the village, that hunger was kept at bay by keeping a pig at the end of the garden for family use and, of course, getting all that could be grown from the cottage plots.

In 1919 there is a reference in the Parish Council minutes to the cost of putting a memorial in the Church, to those who lost their lives during the war. It cost £103 with £10 architect's fees. We set out below more details of those who served from this parish, with an indication as to where and when they lost their lives.

Some details of their service, and in some cases their deaths, have been pieced together from the Commonwealth War Graves Commission records, discussions with descendants, relatives, friends and others who remembered them. For some in this record that follows, familiar or nicknames have been used.

Humphrey Warwick Arden, aged 25, son of the vicar of Whiteparish.

Robert James Cottrell.

Frank Chalk, aged 23, son of Thomas and Matilda Chalk of Sansomes Farm, believed killed in France 29th November 1918.

Samuel Reuben Collins.

George Dibden.

William Charles Elkins, aged 18, son of John and Selina Elkins of Hop Gardens, believed killed in France 10th August 1918.

Thomas Charles Evershed, aged 39, believed killed in France or Belgium 4th October 1917.

William Gilbert.

Frank Goulding, aged 37, Merchant Navy, son of Joshua and Hannah Goulding of Malt Houses, believed to have been torpedoed off the Irish Coast, on his way home aboard the SS Ausonia.

Frank Jerred, aged 29, son of John and Mary Jerred of 'The Street' killed in action aboard H.M.S. Good Hope 1st November 1914.

Charles King, aged 20, son of Edward and Agnes King of Stock Lane, Landford. He is buried in All Saints Churchyard.

Herbert Noble.

Harry Thomas Spare, killed whilst rescuing wounded comrades.

Alfred Stone and Walter Stone.

Walter Stride, aged 30, son of William and Fanny Stride and husband of Edith May Stride of Manor Farm, Cowesfield, died of pneumonia in hospital in Baghdad, 27th December 1917.

Edgar Sturmey.

Edgar Runyard.

Charles Russell

Ernest Edward Young, aged 32, Merchant Navy, son of Frederick Young of the New Inn, believed to have been killed aboard the hospital ship H.M.H.S. Glenart Castle when it was torpedoed by U Boat 56 in the Bristol Channel, en route from Newport, Wales to Brest.

In addition the following are believed to have served during World War 1: -

Alexander Batten.
Charlie Beauchamp, also served in WW2.
'Snowball' Beauchamp.   William Bell.
Fred Bennett.   Harry Bennett
Hubert Bennett.   Fred Billett.
George Brinson.   Reginald Burden.
Fred Chalk.
Jim Chant, who also served in the Boer War.
Arthur Cleverley, who also served in WW2.
William Cobern.
Clem Collins.   George Collins.
Hubert Collins.   Arthur Dibden.
Harold Drake.   Francis Duner.
Harry Dyer.   Walter Dyer.
Edmund Elkins.   John Elkins.
Bob Everill, his son is believed to have served in WW2.
Edward Fuller.   John Fuller.
William Fulford.   Tom Hamblin.
Charles Hayter.   W. Hopkins.
Ernest Light.
Henry Maltby, who was killed in WW 2.
Bill Newman.   Mike Pearce.
Frank Rogers.   Frank Snelgar.
William Spare.   Victor Stone.
Charlie Stride.   George Stride.
Albert Woodford.   Frank Young.

World War 2, 1939-1945 - The first indication that the Parish had of war coming was via the Parish Council in April 1937. A meeting was called to discuss the need for air raid shelters within the village. According to the minutes the public meeting was not well attended. It would seem, reading between the lines, that the meeting was not well focused, for the Council was asked to write for more information from the County. So far we have not been able to find out where the air-raid warden's command post was situated.

Pill box built on the boundary of the Naval Munitions Store, Dean Hill

Another indication that war loomed was that construction began in 1937 of the Naval Munitions stores at Dean. Part of the boundary touched on this Parish. It would appear that the work involved in the construction was beneficial to folk in the surrounding area. After the Irish workers who had been brought over to construct tunnels under the Downland had finished their work, carpenters, electricians, railwaymen and others were needed in ever increasing numbers to run the stores. The increasing cash flow to the Parish must have been very welcome indeed. Work was on the doorstep and the need to go to Southampton or Salisbury to work decreased.

In 1938 the first conscripts were called up, who they were we do not know, but at the end of this account the names of all who served from this village have been listed.

As is well documented it was not until May 1940 that the Nation became aware of its frightful position. The fall of France and the possible invasion of this Country forced Whiteparish, by July of that year, to establish a Home Guard unit in common with most areas in Britain. It was under the control of Major Martin who lived near Broxmore House. As far as we can find out they had a horsebox as a HQ positioned near Ashmore pond, the group had at least two twelve bore guns and each man had a truncheon. At night during the rest of the summer two men patrolled towards Pepperbox, two above Alderstone farm, two at Gatmore and in fact at any large open area that German gliders or parachutists might land. Gradually the units all over the country began to receive more modern weapons. When Melchett Court became one of the main factories building Spitfire fighter planes, the number of men in all the home guard units in the area increased dramatically. One chap recalls how he was made a sergeant but was then called up for the army only two weeks later. It must be remembered that these men not only patrolled at night but had their own work to do during the day, for example, a baker or a dairyman had to leave his post at 4.30 a.m to set off for his work. One or two people we have interviewed and who lived near the boundary of the parish did not like the major in charge and managed to join the Landford or Sherfield English Home Guards.

Around July 1940 regular army units began to appear in the village. We have references to them sleeping under trees at Cowesfield Green. These troops were a unit of the Transport Corps who had the task of servicing the staff cars of the 8th Corps HQ stationed at Melchett Court, this corps had the task of defending the beaches from the east of Portsmouth to Dorset. It must be remembered that after the losses at Dunkirk the troops available were a 'rag bag' army with very little in the way of equipment. The mechanics of the Transport Group, according to the late colonel Terry Sharman, who came with them in 1940, were hard pressed to keep cars on the road. They used the pit belonging to Mr Bailey, the bus owner, which was in a shed, which can still be seen in a garden between the Triangle and the A27. (See reference to this in Col. Sharman's memories).

What was once a sleepy village almost overnight became alive for better or worse!

Cowesfield House was taken over by the army during the summer of 1940, and when the Americans arrived in 1941, Broxmore House was commandeered for their use.

THE SALISBURY AND WINCHESTER JOURNAL, FRIDAY, OCTOBER 14, 1949

Cowesfield House, Whiteparish, the 30-room mansion which was formerly the home of the late Mr. W. F. Lawrence, once Postmaster-General, and which is to be demolished. Unoccupied since the war, its boundaries are still skirted by rolls of barbed wire as a reminder of Allied military requisition. First stages of demolition will be on Wednesday when everything within the walls—and some outside—will be auctioned. Six thousand square feet of flooring and 100 doors are among the listed items. When these have been removed demolition contractors will begin work on the mansion's skeleton.

Cowesfield House showing barbed wire protection

As far as damage from enemy action is concerned only two bombs fell within the parish. A small bomb at the junction of Dean Lane and Fortyacre Lane, and a land mine, a rather nasty affair, at Merry Orchard mushroom farm. It is said that the crater was still visible until recently. There is also a report of a high explosive bomb falling at Landford Wood.

During interviews and tape recordings we have been able to get a flavour of life in the village during the war years. We set out below some of the comments made to us.

Mrs Taylor was a Land Girl called up for war work, she had the option of either going into a factory or in the Land Army or joining the forces. Her home had been in South East London and she had never been away from home before. Directions came to her to go to Whiteparish, and Mr Hamblyn landlord of the Kings Head Inn met her at the station. She had never been in a pub before and had no idea that she was going to live in one, it must be remembered that before the war very few ladies went into a pub unaccompanied and then only occasionally with a husband.

As beer was in short supply in those years a pub was only opened at weekends, however, the landlord made sure he kept the locals supplied. When the Americans came along the beer situation improved, possibly due to political influence.

Mrs Taylor efforts to talk about the jobs she was doing on the farm caused much leg pulling by the locals, her task on the farm at Brickworth was to help with the dairy herd and she worked six days a week. Threshing was the task she hated most, especially the barley ricks for the awns (the stiff bristles on each barley head) would get right into her clothes and cause the most awful rash and itching. Her eyes would fill with dust from the threshing machine, and at night she found her socks so full of awns that she often had to burn them. After a year or two she could almost any task given to do with the cows and calves, but her first effort at driving a van ended in her hitting a tree and never being asked to drive again.

One of her tasks she had to do on her day off was her own laundry; this was done in a bucket supplied by the landlady.

Two other girls lived with her in the Kings Head; both of them worked in the woods with Mr Noble, a forester. Their homes were in Andover and Southampton and they could go home at weekends. Mrs Taylor only managed to go home once a year.

Mrs Elsie Portnall was a cook for Doctor Wilson Smith who lived in Alderstone House. She believes that incendiary bombs were dropped at Brickworth and remembers the Landford Wood high explosive bomb killing two people. She also recalls that high up on the downs at Whelpley Farm there was a bombing practice range used by the RAF. Another of her memories is that always one of the family would stay in the front porch of the house during air raids and, if the German bombers got too close for comfort everybody would rush for their air raid shelter. As their house was very close to the A36 the continual movement of tanks and troop carriers caused such vibrations that the roof of their house was damaged.

Mrs McPhail gives a very good account of the war years she remembers going for a walk with friends, on the Sunday war was declared. They were all young girls and imagined the Germans coming up the road and wondered what they would do about it. Running into the woods, they felt, was the only solution. The barn at the back of Little Suttons was taken over by the army and many soldiers billeted there. In 1940 Mrs McPhail contracted Diphtheria, and had to go into an isolation hospital in Salisbury. It was during the Battle of Britain and planes fought overhead. If the siren sounded the nurses put all the patients under their beds, as there was no air raid shelter. When she fully recovered she was directed to work at the ammunition store at Dean, stacking shells that came in by rail. She recalls stacking TNT for which she was paid danger money. Her weekly wage, in 1945, was £3. 2s.10d. Plus overtime.

So it was that Whiteparish, like all other parts of the country was busy, one way or another. The farmers struggled on, trying to lift the land out of the effects of the depression years and to produce more food. A large number of men were away in the Services, women helped on the land, in the ammunition dumps or other war work, while the enemy planes droned away most nights with un-synchronized engines, a very unnerving sound. Suddenly the world seemed to come to the quiet village of Whiteparish with American, Canadian, and British troops, after six years of this influence the village began to have a different outlook on life.

The following is a list of names of those who died in World War 2: -

Robert Charlie Beauchamp, aged 20, 10th Battalion Gloucestershire Regiment, brother of Barbara Dear, died of wounds 19th August 1944, buried in Yangon (Rangoon).

Geoffrey Frank Bennett, aged 26, 7th Queen's Own Hussars, twin brother of Edna Hyde, died 25th April 1942, buried in Myanmar, Burma.

Eric Arthur Walter Gallop, husband of Dorothy Gallop, died 2nd May 1941, killed aboard the destroyer HMS Jersey when the ship hit a mine when approaching Malta.

Henry Bradford Maltby, aged 54, Royal Naval Reserve, died 25th December 1940 lost at sea whilst conducting North Atlantic Convoy operations aboard HMS Eaglet II. He also served in World War 1.

Patrick Bruce Bine Ogilvie, aged 34, Royal Air Force fighter pilot, died 11th December 1944, shot down over France.

Arthur George Stokes, Royal Artillery, son of Arthur and Alice Mary Stokes of the 'Fountain Inn', died 15th August 1943, buried in Thailand.

Edward James Mortimer Whittle, aged 26, Royal Air Force, died 11th May 1940 buried in Belgium.

In addition the following are believed to have served in World War 2: -

George Alford.	Jack Alford.
Alec Batten.	
Charlie Beauchamp, also served in World War 1.	
Walter Beauchamp.	Maurice Bennett.
Clive Billett.	Charlie Buxton.
Jim Chant.	
Arthur Cleverley, also served in World War 1.	
Reginald Cobern.	Stephen Cobern.
Philip Dear.	Stuart Dear.
Bob Everill, his father is believed to have served in World War 1.	
Arthur Giles.	Arthur Gritt.
Jack Gritt.	Roy Gritt.
Ron Hammond.	Herbert Hawkins.
Sidney Hayes.	Wilfred Hayes.
Ernest Judd.	Viv Judd.
Norman Keats.	Fred Kemish.
Herbert Kemish.	Reginald Lampard.
Stanley Lampard.	Horace Martin.

Stan Martin.
Geoffrey Morgan.
Douglas Pointer.
Clifford Snelgar.
Tony Stride.
Jack Woodford.

Ben McCrow.
Desmond Pointer.
Ken Simmonds.
Ron Stride.
Viv Stride.

British Legion Meeting in the village hall in 1954

CHAPTER 20

THE LATE COLONEL
TERRY SHARMAN

In May 1940 Col. Sharman was stationed in France. He had been there since war was declared. He joined the Army as a boy soldier when he was 14 years of age. He was attached to a motor transport section of the army.

A few days after the Dunkirk evacuation his unit, who were not involved, being stationed further south, were ordered to march to St Nazaire, the port nearest to their station, which took about four hours. They boarded a ship in the harbour, which was immediately bombed by the Germans and sunk. They spent some time in the water as more bombs fell on other ships. Eventually they were picked up by a destroyer, which was also bombed, and although badly damaged, by using manpower to steer the ship, managed to reach Plymouth.

They were sent to the midlands for reorganisation and to a degree re-equipped. He was made a sergeant and posted with his unit to Whiteparish, around July 1940. They had the task of keeping transport going for the H Q of 8th Corp stationed at Melchet Court whose task was the defence of the South Coast (from German Invasion) from Portsmouth to Dorset. He was in charge of a lorry that contained a lathe and electric welding equipment.

The men had no tents to sleep in, most slept under the trees around Cowesfield common although he was fortunate in being able to find room to sleep in the lorry. The food was mostly meat loaf and bully beef, and was often better than that 'enjoyed' by the civilian population.

It was no easy task keeping the staff cars and trucks on the road for spare parts were in short supply. It was a case of improvising. They used the 'pit' and garage belonging to the village bus so that they could work under the vehicles (part of this garage still exists in a shack in the garden below Col Sharmans house in the 'Triangle'). Their work was mainly on electrical repairs; they had a workshop making bushes for starter motors and generators. They also made valves; British vehicles were not good on valves at that time.

The troops became bored so dances were organised at the village hall. There was no food or drink available but something, cider or whatever, could be obtained over the road at the 'New Inn' (now the 'Parish Lantern'). Beer at that time was 4d (under 2p) per pint. The Dances took place fairly often during the winter, with the popular dances the Quickstep, Waltz, Palais Glide, and Valeta, all 'face to face' dancing. It was at one of these Dances that Col Sharman met his wife. A party of boys and girls used to cycle over from Redlynch and it was after one of these visits that Mrs Sharman was caught by the village policeman for not having a lamp on her bike, the fine was a rather steep £2. (We have since been told that in 1940 a boy of 15 was fined 2/6d, five weeks of his pocket money, for a similar offence.)

The remains of the shed on Bunkers Hill that was a bus garage belonging to Mr Bailey. The inspection pit here was used by the army in 1940 when staff cars of the 8th corps, billeted at Melchet Court, were being serviced

The unit moved the next Spring to Downton and then again to Salisbury to ensure that the enemy did not know where the H.Q.was situated.

After a life time in the army Col Sharman and his wife retired back to Whiteparish 24 years ago, his last years in the army were spent in Wilton with U K Land Forces.

Army Pay in 1939 - Private 2/-(10p) a day, Lance Corporal 6/-(30p) a day. Soldier Artificer started at 10/3d (51p) a day. Captain 16/9d (90p) a day, Engineer Captain paid more, marriage allowance (plus one child) £4 a week.

CHAPTER 21

MRS PORTNALLS MEMORIES OF THE VILLAGE

1920's - 1930's

The flower show was held annually at Melchet Court in which all villages in the area took part.

Curfew bell from the church tower rang every evening at 8.00 p.m. (originally to aid travellers). Many village children had to be home before it rang or they could be in trouble.

Gilbert Giles (my grandfather) who lived at Highfield, Romsey Road was a local builder or Maintenance man; he also owned a farm.

Thomas Giles (my great uncle) who lived in Cowesfield Nursery, Romsey Road ran a market garden, supplying the local area, also supplying flowers for weddings and wreaths.

Mr and Mrs Lockyer ran the petrol pump and car/bicycle repair garage. Also selling paraffin, confectionery etc. (situated opposite the Melchet (village) hall). Mr Lockyer was also the church organist.

I remember the Melchet hall being built in approximately 1928. This was given to the village by Lady Mond. Before that the area of the hall and what is now Green Close was allotments.

The main road through the village was tarmac but the lanes like Newton and Dean were just gravel.

Bill Bailey at the Green had two buses, one double decker and one charabanc, supplying the village with transport. He also supplied facilities for charging accumulators for old fashioned wirelesses.

Mr Lampard in HopGardens was the village carrier with his horse and cart. After his retirement Bill Tribble at the Green took over with a motor van.

The village had four inns. The New Inn, now the Parish Lantern, the White Hart, the Kings Head and the Fountain.

Wisteria House during this period was the home of the village doctor and provided the surgery. It was also where one could contact the village nurse.

The newly built village hall 1928

Undertaker/carpenter was Mr Andrews who lived by the Lynches.

The Lynches (middle section) was used as a Reading Room, children's clubs were held there.

The Blacksmith, Mr Lockyer, had his smithy by the Lynches in Dean Lane.

There were three Chapels, Wesleyan in Dean Lane, Methodist in HopGardens and the Plymouth Brethren in the Street in the house named 'the Cottage' next to the Fountain Inn. They later moved to a small building next to the school.

The Woodford family ran the Store and Post Office, they also baked bread. There were two milkmen that delivered milk and there was a butcher in the Street.

I bought my first bicycle at the Cycle shop in Bunkers Hill in a house now known as 'Wickets'.

Starting from the top of Bunkers Hill other places were: -

Pages Shop that sold groceries.
Mrs Brown, sold groceries, I remember taking a jar to her for my mother and she would fill it with treacle for a penny.

Going down the Street: -

Mr Collins, the Cobbler, he also sold milk.
Barbers shop (now Little Rest)
George Till, The Saddler.
Mrs Hayes at the village stores (now the Printers).

Raymond Hayes ran a hardware and cycle shop. He also ran a taxi service. Mrs Hayes played the church organ (after Mr Lockyer).

Early photo of 'The Street' showing the grass verge on each side of the road

Mrs Fuller who ran a small shop from her living room selling Tobacco and Confectionery occupied the last cottage on the left out of the village in Brickworth Road.

On the Southampton Road there was George Dear's garage at Newton Corner with petrol pumps and paraffin. His lorries collected the milk churns in the area.

Also on the Southampton Road (Copse Corner) at what is now Graham's builders yard was the local brickworks, which supplied bricks for many of the local buildings.

Modern picture of 'The Street'

CHAPTER 22

MRS ELSIE PORTNALL
(née GILES)

1920's - 1940's

In these years I lived at Whites Farm, Newton Lane. We were self sufficient foodwise like most families who lived on farms who produced their own meat, vegetables, eggs, butter, cheese, etc. We used oil lamps and candles for lighting and cooked on a solid fuel range. Our water for drinking came from the well. People who did not have their own supply used the community wells in the village. Rainwater was caught and stored in tanks for general use. Washing day was always on a Monday come rain or shine.

Families helped one another, my Grandparents, with other members of the family, lived in the village. We eventually moved to Cletola, Southampton Road, a small holding where the family live to the present day.

Early picture of School House and the school, the school is to the right

At seven years of age, in 1920, I went to Whiteparish School. Mr Faulkner was the headmaster, a very gentle and placid man. He lived, of course, in the School House next to the school and a special treat for his pupils, when good, was letting us into his home to listen to his crystal set. Every Christmas we would receive a gift of an orange and some sweets from the family at Brickworth House.

On Election days we would have a day off school, the locals would get together for fun and play music on the green opposite the school, the local policeman would guard the voting booth.

Once a year a Fair would come to the village, being held in the field opposite the 'White Hart' (the Recreation Ground) the field at that time being owned by the landlord, Bill Tubb who removed his cattle for such a special event. There would be roundabouts, swings, a coconut shy and hoopla.

I went to the Wesleyan Chapel in Dean Lane for Sunday school; we would have outings to Nomansland, Dean Hill and Pepperbox Hill. This seemed a long way in those days, we travelled in horse drawn wagons, always three, one for the girls, one for the boys and the third with guards around for the younger children.

I became a Girl Guide at the age of eleven in Lady Mond's group at Melchett Court.

My childhood days in this village were happy days.

War Time Memories 1940 - 1945

Whiteparish had a home guard; the hut they used was situated in Dean Lane on the right hand side just before Alderstone House. I worked as cook for Doctor Wilson Smith, our village GP at Alderstone, which was then the doctor's surgery.

As far as I can remember the only area of the village that had anything dropped on it by the Germans during the war years was the Brickworth Park area, these were incendiary bombs.

There was a bomb dropped on a cottage in Landford Wood, which sadly killed the two occupants, and a second one came down at Landford Pound, this one failed to explode.

We had a practice bombing range in the village in the Whelpley Farm area to the north of Brickworth Road; very noisy Lancaster Bombers also practised there at night.

The German planes would fly over the village on their way to bomb Bristol, this was very frightening, they seemed to have a special drone which you recognised straight away as they approached.

There was always one of our family in our front porch over night keeping a lookout, any danger we would rush to our air raid shelter.

The movement of very large tanks at night along the main A36 coming and going to Southampton etc. caused great damage to roads and property and was very noisy. Our bungalow (Cletola) actually had its roof damaged by the continuous vibration of the tanks. Troops would march through during day and night, resting every so often by the roadside and during the day stopping in the shade of trees.

There were British, American and Canadian soldiers. Americans were camped in the Earldoms/Landford area. When they saw you out and about with a small child they would often throw bars of chocolate into the child's pram as they passed.

There were British soldiers up at the Cowesfield Park area, and after they were moved out, the Americans moved in. Many British soldiers stayed in the homes of village families.

We all tried to get on with our lives during those years, many women opted for the open air life working on the land and also many women from the village went to do war work at Dean Hill.

CHAPTER 23

MRS BARBARA McRORY'S MEMORIES

Barbara was one of four children of a regular army man and they travelled the world with him. When he became a prisoner of war in Crete the family moved into the Top Lodge of Brickworth House, this was when Barbara was 14 so she did not attend Whiteparish School although her younger siblings did. She went to work for Marks & Spencer in Salisbury, although only 14, and travelled to work on the bus for 1/3d return each day. If the weather was bad, with snow or fog, the store used to allow the staff to leave early to catch an early bus.

She earned 25/- a week, the store used to subsidise a midday meal as the management felt it essential that staff had a good meal at midday.

During the war years there were several Nissan type huts (known as chalets by the residents) in the grounds of Brickworth House in which various families were settled, having left areas which were being bombed, Southampton, Portsmouth and London for example. There was a feeling of real community there.

Mrs McRory remembers the bombing practice range near Whelpley Farm. Also she and other youngsters used to sit and chat in the armoured cars that were parked nearby, until turned out by the soldiers. Mrs McRory also has memories of food rationing. For example, if a family did not need any particular part of the ration, Mr Edmunds, who ran a general store where the sign shop is now, used to offer a different item that was perhaps needed. Life was made as easy as possible.

Dances, held regularly in the village hall, were well attended. A group of youngsters would walk from Brickworth, picking up friends en-route, sometimes including young mothers with babies in prams. Most of the dances had live music but sometimes the music was from 'records' played on Mr Coombs radiogram. Mr Witchell and Mr Coombs both had small dance bands that would play on these occasions. There were also dances at Sherfield English, which were popular, but the dancers had to walk to Sherfield English for them. They also used to attend dances in Romsey. They would go by car with as many people as possible packed in, sitting on laps, all for 2/6d (12.5p) each. Soldiers used to attend these dances and many a marriage followed a meeting at the hall. Sach Noble and Fred Alford ran the dances in the hall at that time. The Americans who were billeted in the district introduced the 'jitterbug' dance to the village.

There were soldiers from the Signals Corps and from the Parachute Regiment, then called the Airborne Division, at Cowesfield; Mrs McRory's husband was from the

Parachute Regiment. There were six landgirls billeted at the 'Kings Head' and several of them married local boys. There was no alcohol at dances but the 'New Inn' was opposite the Hall and was much used.

After the war, much of the social side of life was connected with speedway racing. There were several Speedway bikes at Brickworth. They used to go into Southampton for the races on their own motor bikes, Mrs McRory can remember travelling at 90mph on the old Southampton Road.

The young couple moved into one of the thatched cottages behind the Lynches (they are now demolished) for a rent of 5/- per week, paid to Mr Kemish on behalf of Jessica Lawrence deceased (!) They had a kitchen with no running water, a living room and two bedrooms. The toilet was in a shed in the garden the 'waste' from which had to be buried at the back of their large garden; there was no electricity of course. Every Sunday Mrs McRory would visit her mother in Brickworth, and give her husband a little privacy to have a bath in the kitchen with water, drawn from a local well and warmed on a range which burned wood. The wood was collected all through the year and stored in a shed in the large garden that the cottage had. The lighting was paraffin lamps; Jack Edmunds delivered the paraffin every Friday.

Wash days were hard work as, once again, all water was heated on the range. Butter was kept in a tin sunk into the ground. Meat was kept in a meat safe hanging or standing in the coolest place in the house. The milkman delivered milk to the house.

Mr McRory worked for Halfords and Barbara continued to work for Marks & Spencer until her daughter was born in 1948. She had a 'home delivery' with Dr Jepson and Nurse Witchell in attendance. There was no National Health Service at the time so the fee for the doctor was 10 guineas and for the nurse £3. After the birth Nurse Witchell took Mrs McRory to be churched, something that is rarely done today. Orange juice and cod liver oil was available for young children as a boost to their vitamin intake but Barbara cannot remember where the collection point was.

Mrs McRory considers the village to be a very friendly place, in her early married life, when food was in short supply, any excess food produced in gardens would be shared out. This would also apply if a pig were killed, as there were no fridges or freezers, the meat had to be cured or shared out among friends of the pig owners.

Mrs McRory left the village in 1959 when her husband's job took them to Cheltenham but her mother moved from Brickworth to the 'old folks' bungalows in the village and her brother, David Crombie, still lives in Whiteparish although, as he puts it, he has been a 'wanderer' having moved to Downton for a while before coming back to Whiteparish.

CHAPTER 24

MRS IRIS McPHAIL'S MEMORIES.

Mrs McPhail's father, Mr English, was a Londoner but became a baker in Winton, Bournemouth, and her mother (Mrs English) started work in a farmhouse over the top of Dean Hill. Having spent her 'afternoons off' at home in Whiteparish Iris McPhail's grandmother used to walk with her daughter (Iris McPhail's mother) to the top of the hill carrying a lantern and as the young girl headed off across fields to the farm would call out regularly 'are you all right?' and was answered until the farm was reached. Mothers were worried for their daughters even in those days. Eventually she went into service in Bournemouth and that is where Iris's parents met.

At the outbreak of World War 1 her father had to join the army where he helped to look after the horses and was eventually invalided out. Meanwhile her mother returned home to live with grandmother bringing with her Iris McPhail's eldest sister, eventually there were six children in the family, Iris being No5. The young mother and baby were able, in time, to move into the cottage next door to grandmother on 'the Green'. The cottages were a group of eight thatched cottages owned by the church and eight slate- roofed cottages owned by Mr Knapman of Tytherly. The rent was 2/6d per week or £5 per year with a rebate of 2/6d if the rent was paid on the day due.

An early photograph of the thatched cottages on 'the Green'

When father was invalided out of the Army he was obliged to work on the land as 'War Work' and after the war went into the building trade and worked on the Melchet Estate for Lord and Lady Mond. Iris has memories of her father receiving a bonus of £5 with which he bought a pair of brown brogue shoes and also some little presents for the children, hers being a pair of white sandals which he hid in the toes of his new shoes for her to find.

The family regularly attended the Flower Shows at Melchet Court. They used to walk via footpaths from the 'New Inn' and Parkwater up to the house. If the family had enough money they would catch a bus instead.

Father was a keen gardener, and also had one of the allotments; these ran from the Green down towards Romsey. These allotments provided most of the family's vegetables for the year but watering was difficult as all the water came from wells in the village. The 'New Inn' now called 'The Parish Lantern', was a great attraction to the men. The wives would be sitting, chatting, on the front doorsteps of the house and the men supposedly working out the back had a handy footpath leading to the Pub! The family kept and bred rabbits and hens that provided eggs and were kept for meals later as was quite usual. They also made wine, dandelion, elderberry and other fruits were used, and the resulting wine, especially the dandelion was thought to keep arthritis at bay. Mrs McPhail remembers that the Sunday papers were delivered from Romsey and the 'paperman' who called on them last on his round, always went home by bus having enjoyed a large glass of dandelion wine. Mrs McPhails mother worked at the poultry farm plucking and dressing birds. The farm was sited each side of Dean Lane and employed several people from the village. Mrs McPhail remembers the land was eventually used as a market garden and later bungalows were built on it.

In the 1930's there was a footpath which led from Dean Lane near Alderstone House (which the Doctor Wilson Smith occupied) down through the allotments to the 'New Inn' (now the 'Parish Lantern').

Mrs McPhail left school at 14 and took employment as a maid for three ladies living in the White House off Dean Lane; she left there hurriedly after the first day because she could not abide the cats in the house.

Her next employment was as 'mothers help' to Mrs Dawkins who had recently had a baby and who ran a Sweet Shop from 'Little Suttons'. Later the house became a lodging house for men, most of them working at Melchet Hall, doing major building work there. She would help with the laundry, preparing meals and clearing up afterwards, but her main job was to care for the baby. Her wages were 10/- a week. She believes the lodgers paid £1 per week (later 30/-) for their weekly board. Mrs McPhail's future husband was one of the boarders; he had come down from Scotland for a period of recuperation following serious illness, and never went back!

The social life for young men and women in the village was limited but fun. There were dances held in the village hall, with live music provided by a village band, led by Mr Lockyer and later in war time by musicians from the forces billeted locally. There was the Band of Hope meetings on Mondays and on Wednesdays there was an evening devoted to girls skills, which Mrs McPhail did not join. There were Cubs and Scouts, Brownies and Girl Guides groups all well attended. The Scouts having Jamborees in Salisbury, local boys going into Salisbury on the Bailey's bus. Chapel was attended three time each Sunday with a sweet if the children arrived early whilst Mr Lockyer was lighting up the fires, there were apples in the autumn. Her brother joined the Church choir, as there was a penny to be earned for each service attended

She continued to work for Mrs Dawkins but at 18 she had to join either war work or the forces. She was drafted into war work having failed to obtain farm work. Mrs McPhail remembers the declaration of war being announced on the wireless set. These sets were run on accumulators, a type of battery, which had to be charged each week. This had to be done through Mr Bailey, who ran the bus service, and cost sixpence.

The Tank Corp quickly requisitioned the barn at the back of 'Little Suttons' for army use and many soldiers were billeted in the village.

In early 1940 Mrs McPhail was diagnosed as suffering from Diphtheria and was taken to Old Sarum Isolation Hospital. She spent seven and a half weeks there. The treatment consisted of at least one large injection, which she recalls was awful, and then hot treated gauze was wrapped around her throat and bandaged on. She was made to lie flat, no pillows. She could not eat or drink for some time. Whilst in hospital she was told that Whiteparish had been bombed, a landmine had fallen in Cowesfield Woods and a bomb had fallen on a bungalow in Dean Hill. She can recall the planes going overhead during the Battle of Britain. If a siren sounded, whilst she was in hospital, the nurses would lift the patients from their beds and place them under the bed, this was all the protection they had. Whilst in hospital she could receive no visitors, only see them through a glass screen, but her friend, later to become her husband, David, visited the hospital regularly and during that time he proposed. They kept their engagement secret because it was felt her mother would not approve, presumably because she would be considered too young.

As soon as she regained her health Mrs McPhail started war work at East Dean which involved stacking shells into tunnels. Train or truck brought in the shells. She was also involved in stacking TNT, which was a dangerous substance. This was done by hand as no machinery could be used in case sparks should occur. In 1945 Mrs McPhail's wages were £3 2s 10d a week with overtime extra, still doing war work.

Mr and Mrs McPhail married in 1944, and lived for some time with Mrs Dawkins in her crowded house. They spent their honeymoon in Southampton, which was at that time very badly damaged by earlier bombing. Mr McPhail did not go into the forces his previous illness had made service life impossible.

By 1945 Mrs McPhail was again unwell, but the doctor put it down to 'general debility', so she continued her war work but eventually she had to give in. Subsequently it was found that she had a peptic ulcer, which involved another eight weeks in hospital.

On being allowed home again Mrs McPhail had extra rations of milk (2.5 pints per day) and eggs. She was off sick for a whole year. For the time she was in hospital her husband had to pay £1 per week to the Almoner. Money was very short, what with paying lodging, fares to and from hospital, and the £1 per week. In August 1945 Mr and Mrs McPhail's first home was a thatched cottage on Bunkers Hill, one room upstairs, one downstairs, no water or electricity inside. The rent was 2/6d per week

(12.5 pence). For some time she did no outside work. Mr McPhail was by then a painter and decorator. Mrs McPhail has an invoice for work done for Mr Till, the saddler, £14 10/- for painting the house and shop. She also has references to the cost of materials, one quart of gloss white paint - 6/9d, a gallon, of green gloss paint - 15/-, 7lb of distemper green or white - 5/6d, 14lb primrose distemper 10/9d, these prices were for goods and services in 1946.

Eventually as her health returned Mrs McPhail returned to work for 2 or 3 days each week looking after two small children in their house, keeping their nursery clean, and taking them for walks. She earned 10/- per week. Pressure was put on them to move out of their cottage but they had nowhere else to go. They went to Court but lost their case so moved into the bungalow that Mrs McPhail lives in today

CHAPTER 25

THE MEMORIAL GROUND STORY

To make it clear to those who may not be aware, the Memorial Ground is for all intents and purposes a village playing field. The two most powerful groups in the charitable trust controlling the ground being the Football and Cricket clubs. Villagers have access to it for walking but nowadays no dogs are allowed in.

It is interesting to read in various minutes of the council how this came about. We have to go back even before the parish became involved, for we have heard in an interview recorded on tape, how the Cricket Club played on this field when it was part of the tenancy of the 'White Hart' public house. Mr McCrow tells how as a very small boy back in the 1930's, he was given the task, when the teams were having tea in the 'pub', of keeping the cows off the pitch, for which he was given sixpence. He tells us this was greatly appreciated for pocket money was non existent in those days. It seems that at this time, the Football Club played on a field alongside Newton Lane, when it was not flooded.

Certainly around 1934, Parsonage meadow was sometimes used for sporting fixtures by kind permission of the tenant of Alderstone farm. This is when the Parish Council began to take an interest. They very much wanted this field for the village as a recreational area. As far as we can find out this idea was gleaned from the Home Office who at this time were pushing the idea of garden cities and parks. Miss Bristow of Broxmore House owned the field in question. It was agreed to get the field valued by a Salisbury valuer and then to approach the owner to find out if she would accept an offer and sell. As far as we can make out it was valued at £45 an acre and it was 9 acres in size. It was hoped to raise the money within the village. Unfortunately Miss Bristow would not sell and the idea was shelved for the time being. War loomed and gradually parish affairs had to take second place to more life threatening matters, until the war ended in 1945.

As with many, if not all, villages and towns in the country, money was raised to give a great homecoming to the chaps who had been away. Some £500 was raised and at this point the then chairman of the Council, Mr Alford, had the brilliant idea of using this money to buy a field for the village. It would be a sports field, a memorial to those who had been away at war. The wise heads of the parish could see that it was very much better to do this rather than blow the money on one big party, soon forgotten.

By this time Miss Bristow had passed away, so an agreement was reached with her heir, Mr Bristow Bull, around 1947 to buy the field that is now the Recreation Ground. Straightaway a charitable trust was formed and to make sure the ground could not be sold away from the village, the whole village population over 18 years of age, would have to vote by a majority on any changes that might be sought.

Before 1981 four members of the Parish Council and one member from each of the Sports Clubs formed the Trust. In 1981 a chance came to sell part of this ground to the local doctors, Dr Baston being head of the practice, operating from Wisteria House. A great debate took place in the parish as to whether this was a breach of the rules as laid down by the Charity Commissioners. It would seem the debate was fast and furious, from the pulpit and outside the church. A vote was taken and the village decreed that the sale could take place. By now £12000 had come into the coffers of the Trust and it was agreed to take away the responsibilities of the Trust Committee as set out in 1947 and to form another Trust Committee. The new Committee was to comprise eight members, four from the Parish Council, one from each of the Cricket and Football Clubs and two members to be voted in by the other members. In effect this Committee can administer the ground and the money invested, but cannot give permission for the sale of the ground or other projects that might be put forward unless these are in the interests of the existing sports clubs. To change this rule again all those over 18 years of age in the Parish must be called upon to vote. It is not only the EEC that demands a referendum.

Mr David Wills, a solicitor living at that time in the village, kindly supplied much of the information involving the Trusts, and indeed played a very large part in setting up the new Trust. He recounts how the original documents to buy the ground were signed in Ivy Cottage, and the documents for the new sale and Trust some forty years later were signed in the same house.

The pavilion and youth club hut 1999

The children's play area 1999

CHAPTER 26

MRS EVELYN AND
MR BEN McCROW'S MEMORIES

Evelyn was born in the 'White Hart' public house. Her father died when she was quite young, her mother continued as licensee. Cows were kept in buildings behind the 'White Hart'. Evelyn helped her mother to churn the butter and delivered the milk on her bicycle. Evelyn claims that this was her only job at the time, and she did not ever pull a pint. The cows were sent across the road to feed in what is now the recreation ground. When cricket matches were played on this field it was Ben's job to keep the cows off the pitch when the teams were having tea at the 'White Hart'. Often a party of people came from Southampton and Evelyn's mother catered for them in a big marquee in the field

Strong and Co of Romsey owned the 'White Hart' and when the lease expired Evleyn's mother and children were transferred to the 'Kings Head' also in the 'Strong Country'. Four or five cows were then kept at the 'Kings Head'. When milking was finished they were driven up Dean Lane to a field named 'Nunn's Park'. Water for the cows was obtained from Ashmore Farm.

A pleasure in those days was dancing in the main part of the school to piano music played by Mr Lockyer. On other occasions Mr Lockyer used his big shed which had a lovely wooden floor. Sometimes a band provided the music.

Practice rifle shooting took place on the rifle range, now the site of the village hall. Lord Melchet donated the money for the hall, which was built in 1928. Ben and Evelyn went to Band of Hope meetings on Monday nights. There was a summer outing to Bramshaw in a wagon supplied by Mr Gay of Alderstone farm, a devout Chapel man. He owned some twenty cart horses, and Evelyn claims that Mr Gay was the first person to have a motor car in Whiteparish. It was an open topped 'Swift'. Also remembered was the 'New Inn' (now the 'Parish Lantern') and the allotments on the other side of the road. In Common Road, New Forest ponies were often to be found in people's gardens spoiling their well tended plants and flowers. Off Common Road in Clay Street, the former Wesleyan Chapel building still stands, on the right past the two bungalows and two cottages. On the further side is the late Len Cobern's house.

Evelyn with Vera Woodford, Iris Slade and Gower Slade attended Sunday evening service at Whiteparish Church (and here is a challenge for us today!) Evelyn said "if we did not go to Whiteparish we walked either to Sherfield English or to Landford for a change".

Early picture of the 'White Hart' showing Jess Hamblyn and Sam Winter at the back and Flo Howerd and Agnes Hamblyn in the front

Ben was born in 1906, a Scottish name perhaps but his father was a Londoner. Ben attended Chapel three times on a Sunday. There were two telephones in the village, one in the doctor's house and the other at the Post Office. If Ben happened to be in the Post Office when a telegram came in, Vera would ask him to deliver it for which he was well rewarded. Ben also delivered the 'Echo' newspaper for the princely sum of 1d per week. He left school at 13 and went to work in the sawmill where 30 or more people from Whiteparish either worked or were connected with the mill. There were two sawmills in Whiteparish one on Holmere Common and the other quite nearby on the site that is now Grahams in Common Road. The sawmill to start with had an old steam engine until it was replaced by a smart diesel engine. Ben's pay packet dated 14th November 1941 when working at the Agricultural Chalk Company allowing for National Insurance of 11d and Income Tax of 7 shillings amounted to £4. 4s. 1d.

People from the village had to walk to Brickworth Corner to pick up a bus to Southampton or Salisbury. Later Bill Bailey ran a bus service from Whiteparish. Evelyn recalls walking to Dean with her mother and sister to catch a train to Salisbury

CHAPTER 27

HEALTH THROUGH THE CENTURY

Recollections of Doctors Daphne & John Baston.

Doctor Allington was appointed Doctor in the village in 1902 and on his giving up the practice in 1907 was succeeded by Doctor Henry Case. From 1911 - 1920s Doctor William Hopkins tended to the needs of the village whilst between the two world wars two doctors (brothers), Doctors Stuart & R Vivian were the village doctors. Doctor Wilson-Smith, who was also a keen botanist, ran his surgery from the newly built 'Ashmore House' between 1938 and 1945. Doctor W B Jepson MC took over at this point and was running the practice from 'Wisteria House' when the Bastons arrived in Whiteparish in 1963.

An early picture of Wisteria House

Dr. Jepson lost a leg in the First World War whilst serving in the R.A.M.C. It is thought the injury occurred on the Somme. Patients also thought he was a somewhat adventurous motorist especially coming out on to the A27. As a patient remarked to Dr John Baston "Providence has been very good to him". In fact it was never heard of him being involved in any accident, unlike his successor who met a milk van head on in a very muddy Newton Lane when driving a Mini. The milk van was towed away!

The Doctors Baston arrived on January 1st 1963, an arctic winter many residents may recall. They dropped the children John Richard aged 10, Caroline aged 5 and James aged 2 with Granny Baston at Yeovil, just to cover the move. They were destined to be there for more than a week. A poor weather forecast made the Bastons change their plans and drive back to Birmingham through the night. They just managed to get through a blizzard in the Cotswolds before the roads became impassable. Next day most roads, including the A36 at Pepperbox Hill were blocked so they came with the furniture vans via Oxford and Newbury. There was more snow to come and there was no thaw until March.

The appointment to the practice at Whiteparish was only confirmed late in December, so there was no question of looking for accommodation. They just had to accept the massive Georgian house (Wisteria House) that had been home and surgery to the local doctors for most of the previous one hundred years. Their predecessor, who owned it, was retiring on that day January 1st. He was kindness itself. He was asking a modest price and suggested that they cut out legal formalities and just give him a cheque. He seemed quite surprised that they needed a mortgage!

The house was splendid but it required much work. There were no gutters, and the survey described the back of the coach house, 'as collapsing'. The electric wiring was original; dating from the time that the house had its own private generator, and was so unsafe that the surveyor hammered wooden plugs into the two point system until the house could be rewired. There was no gas in the village, so the heating was either oil or wood. The bedrooms, seven of them, had beautiful 18th and 19th century iron fireplaces. The doctors contemplated lighting fires, but they did not appear to have been used for years and it was thought that it might set the whole place alight. At least that would have made them warmer! The drainage was to a septic tank in the garden; the pump blocked most weeks and unblocking it was quite a performance. There was an Aga in the house, a solid fuel Aga, which also heated the water. Although most of the pipes in the house were frozen, this supply seemed immune. The Aga was in a massive farmhouse kitchen, a grand room, which was to be the nerve centre of the family and the practice. Dr. John made a splendid table for the room from a door bought locally. The Aga dominated the doctor's lives it seemed to take a malevolent delight in going out at the most inconvenient moments; it seemed to forecast impending disaster. It took several people several hours to coax the Aga to relight with paper, firelighter, wood, charcoal and finally coke by which time the kitchen would be black with soot. But the Aga seemed never to fail during frequent power cuts.

As the doctors moved in, their predecessor, unable to leave because of the snow, sat by the Aga and directed the furniture men. The new owner's furniture was coming in through the back door and Dr. Jepsons going out through the front door, well mostly! Dr. Daphne is sure that some of it went round several times. Once Dr Jepson's van was full he asked them to keep the rest of his 'bits and pieces' saying he would send for it later. Amongst those things left was a lovely old piano, which was to give them much pleasure. Also there were First World War puttees, coronation decorations, stone hot water bottles, picture frames, gas masks, a skeleton, tin hats, two artificial legs and hundreds of old copies if the 'Times'. Three days later Dr Jepson was persuaded to move to the 'White Hart'. He seemed reluctant to leave the old house but it was essential that the new family should have the ability to move round the house freely especially as Dr. John was holding surgery in the house.

The existing consulting room was at the side of the house with a door leading to a drive where there was a galvanised lean-to with a single row of chairs awaiting patients. As if to prove that the house needed much attention there was an occasion when a chair, with occupant, went through the floor.

It had been decided that as far as possible John would look after the practice for the first few days while Daphne tackled the house. The really onerous thing about general practice is that it never stops. John had a formidable task, trying to find patients over appalling roads, covered in deep snow, in a new area with houses not numbered and sometimes not even named. They were on call 24 hours a day, every day, and it was to be nearly twelve years before they had the assistance of another partner.

The nearest neighbouring practices are five and seven miles away at Broughton and Downton. The doctors Baston were to become firm friends with the doctors in these practices and would occasionally take surgeries for them but geography of the area prevented night duties being shared which meant that either Daphne or John would have to be on duty 24 hours a day.

The practice was small, rural, exactly the type that was wanted but was it viable? The local N.H.S. administrator thought is probably was. There was supposed to be 1100 patients. A flat annual rate was paid for each one. The patients were very scattered and had been notified of the new doctors' appointment, but when the final count was complete, having excluded those who had moved, died or could not be traced, the number was down to 900, certainly not viable. It was thought that it would not be "all beer and skittles" and it seemed that a spot of good luck was needed. It was not long after this that. Dr Whitehead of Downton phoned to say that he had many patients in Whiteparish who lived nearer to the Whiteparish surgery than his and if any wished to change they could do so with his blessing. This was kindness to two struggling young people but medicine then was not about competition. Dr Parr of Broughton, who had hoped that Whiteparish might be served medically from West Dean, as a branch of his practice, swallowed his disappointment and phoned to wish the new doctors well.

The lean-to on the side of the house, which was the waiting room, had a corrugated iron roof and even with oil stove burning it was so cold inside that the water in the flower vase froze. Few would visit the doctor because anyone passing could see who was waiting, and it made splendid village gossip. Soon the entrance hall became the waiting room and the lean-to was taken down. By 1965 the stable block, which in living memory had housed a stable lad, employed to saddle the doctor's horse, had become the surgery. The old wash room, which still contained a galvanised bathtub, a substantial fireplace and screens for Victorian modesty, made a peerless dispensary. The doctors were aware that they might have been criticised for altering the old building but hoped that they were working with sensitivity.

It had been a condition of the doctors' appointment that they should dispense medicines for all patients living more than a mile from the nearest chemist and that was virtually all their patients. They would need regular visits to Boots the chemist. The doctors took it in turn to do the school run to Salisbury. They would drive in through St Ann's Gate, which was open to traffic in those days, drop the children at various schools, go out through High Street Gate, park outside Boots, there were no yellow lines then, and collect the drugs needed. They are very proud of the fact that they actually supplied drugs to Boots on one occasion. Whoever was doing the 'drug run', would make any visits on that side of the practice on the way back to Whiteparish. They found it was an extraordinary privilege to go into people's homes.

The doctors wondered how they were going to run their practice. What did the patients want? What did their children need? What were they actually trying to do? They had a vast family house in which the priority was a safe playroom for the children and, as the house would be used by many people, a foolproof way of preventing the children form getting on to the road. They needed a telephone in their bedroom and a night bell. Their predecessor had relied on the traditional method of patients throwing a pebble at the window if they required a doctor at night. They needed someone to be with the children if they both had to go out. Daphne could work in the surgery and John could make the visits but that didn't allow for the urgent call or the phone to be answered when the children were in the house.

Surgery hours were published and the doctors would thank patients who attended at those times, but the doctors made it a policy to see patients at any time. They ran a separate mother and baby clinic which kept the sick away from the healthy children. They also thanked patients who requested visit before 10 am as that helped them to rationalise the home visits. They kept branch surgeries at West Dean, West Tytherly and the Lamb Inn at Nomansland. They had a policy for repeat prescriptions and they carried a basic stock of drugs in the car to dispense when they visited the sick.

Among Dr Jepson's belongings, that were still in the attic some years after the move, was a stout wooden box which, since they had been told by Dr Jepson to use anything they needed, they decided to make into a portable dispensary. In addition to conventional medical bags they each carried emergency kits which consisted of intravenous fluids and giving sets, tracheostony sets, accident triangles and eventually green flashing lights that could go on the car roof, and of course an emergency midwifery bag. There was a flying squad for 'midder' with a consultant, an anaesthetist and a nursing sister. Doctor Daphne can recall two occasions when they probably saved a mother's life; this was the days before the accident flying squad. They were frequently called out to road traffic accidents at the notorious Brickworth Corner junction of the A27/A36. Daphne still has horrific memories of the worst of these accidents, one, especially, when a Mini van full of people had been hit side on and some of the occupants flung out. When the accident seemed serious both doctors would go to the scene and as they were the nearest they usually arrived before the police. One immediate difficulty on a dark night is to prevent other vehicles running into the casualties or wreckage. The immediate priority is to establish a patients pulse and airway and then decide if they are fit to be moved to the grass verge out of danger. It was always a great relief to the doctors when the police arrived to control the traffic and to summon the ambulance. All police, even the very young, who were unused to these horrors, were exemplary. Ambulance crews are the 'salt of the earth' and the doctors suspect that they are under appreciated. Hospitals and police are sometimes criticised for the delay in telling relatives about accident victims but identification is low on the list of priorities when efforts are being made to save lives.

In 1963 Whiteparish was still a traditional labour intensive farming community. Many families had lived here for many generations and doctors wondered how they would be received, especially Daphne as the first women doctor in the village. Late one evening, soon after they took up the practice, several polite, but rather drunk young men, knocked on the door of Wisteria House carrying a friend who had fallen through a window. He was bleeding profusely from a long cut in his forearm, and one of the men was promptly sick on the doorstep. Daphne chose the most sober looking to come in with the patient and, giving the other three a mop and bucket, told them to clear up the mess, firmly shutting the door on them, whilst she stitched the arm. Next morning the step was spotless the blood had gone and much of the snow had been cleared away. Fortunately the arm healed well. This incident seemed to break the ice.

The practice grew very quickly. By this time the doctors had recruited Mrs Barbara Dear to act as receptionist and dispenser. Within 18 months they had 1800 patients. Their concerns changed from solvency to coping with the demands of the practice and giving their children a reasonable amount of time. It was impossible to go out as a family, but they had a glorious spacious family home and patients were always kindness and generosity itself, giving them far more than they could give the patients. This is the experience of many doctors.

So the doctors divided the work into patient care which was shared equally including night calls and bank holidays. Daphne also ran the home and family whilst John managed the finances, administration and the pharmacy. None of this would have been possible without the staff. During the first year Maureen Bates who was very good with the children and a particularly good cook provided help. Then came Barbara Dear who was so versatile, she answered the phone, got out the notes, dispensed, did the washing, helped with the cooking, found the homework, washed the medicine bottles for reuse and occasionally told people off if she considered they were being unreasonable. Over the years she attained the post of Practice Manager, retired and was succeeded by Mrs Elizabeth Carter as Practice Manager in 1993. Sheila Metcalfe joined the staff as Secretary/Receptionist, and proved to have an exceptional instinct for the really urgent case and dealt with patients with great tact.

The new Doctor's surgery being built 1981

The surgery in 1999

In the early 1970's Dr. Peter Claydon joined the practice and on 13th December 1982, Dr's Daphne and John Baston and Dr Claydon moved to a new surgery in Common Road next to the Church. Dr. Rosemary Parry joined the practice in 1983/4. The Doctors Baston retired from the practice in October 1987 and Dr. Christopher Gotham joined in 1989. It was found that the practice needed to be extended and the first extension was built in 1989. The need for more space was because there was an opportunity to provide another consulting room for a training doctor and to have room for a Health Visitor and new library for the Surgery. In 1993 Dr. Isobel Dean joined the practice.

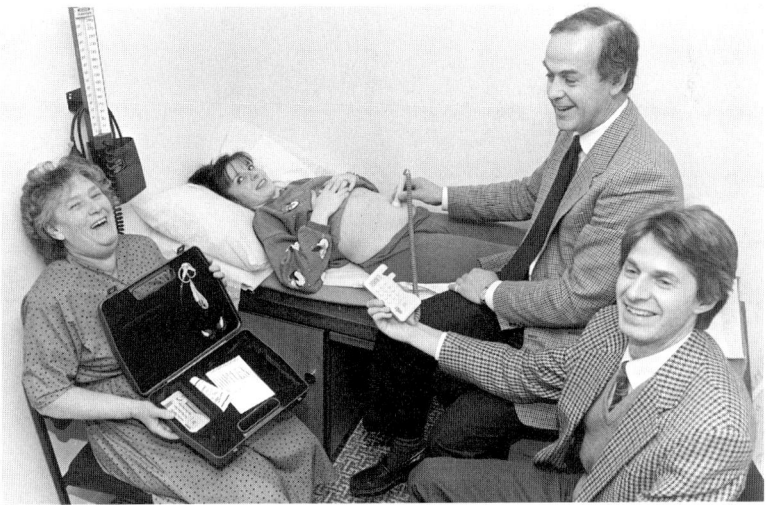

Dr Claydon and Dr Gotham trying out the new baby monitor bought with money raised by Mrs Joan White (left)

Fundholding started for the practice in 1994. Under the fundholding they were able to have physiotherapy in the Surgery and also Chiropody and Counselling.

In 1997 they were able to extend the Surgery still further to provide another consulting room, to improve office facilities and to create more space for the Practice Manager, Secretary, Fundholding and Community Staff (Midwife, Health Visitor and District Nurses).

In June 1999 another partner Martin Essigman, joined the Practice, and the Whiteparish Surgery became a five-partner practice.

The size of the Surgery has more than doubled in the last 26 years. The greatest changes have been the provision of a treatment room with minor surgery facilities, resuscitation facilities and the total computerisation of the medical facilities. The practice now has a computer based information system using electronic links for registration and items of service activity. The great benefit to the village of the change of use of part of the Memorial Ground field to a Surgery site is that the Surgery is able to provide a car park for the village and the Church.

The Sunday School uses the community room and on occasions the Parish Council Committee uses the Surgery as a meeting place. In the absence of Church lavatories, the Surgery has provided cloakroom facilities for Church activities. The wicket gate from the Surgery car park into the churchyard was placed there in memory of Mrs Hersey Morgan by her husband and family.

The Surgery has been a centre for training in General Practice over 35 years.

The Doctors and other staff of the Whiteparish Surgery 1999

CHAPTER 28

RECOLLECTIONS OF NURSING AND MIDWIFERY OVER 40 YEARS

by MRS JOAN WITCHELL Nurse for 40 years

When Joan began work in the village, she made her calls, travelling by bike, in all weathers, going out as far as Nomansland. She has vivid memories of struggling through snow during the winter of 1947 to deliver babies. She had by then acquired a car, but during the really bad weather, she relied on her husband to act as driver.

In 1972 Joan's duties were extended to tending to post-operative patients and the elderly housebound, in addition to her midwifery duties of pre and postnatal care. Her years as a midwife has meant she has helped in the delivery of babies to mothers who were the girls she assisted into the world in her early years.

One of her outstanding memories is of delivering a gypsy baby, by candlelight in the presence of the Gypsy Queen.

Joan has been honoured by receiving the Queen's Silver Jubilee Medal for services to the community. For six years she was Madam Chairman of the Salisbury branch of the College of Midwives. For many years she has served on the Stewardship Committee in Whiteparish, being a 'leading light' in organising the Whiteparish Week each year.

Nurse Witchell standing outside the surgery
at Wisteria House

CHAPTER 29

MEMORIES OF VERONICA ILES
(née PORTNALL)

1955 - 1965

In my teenage years the village seemed smaller and the community seemed friendlier. The younger element was quite well behaved although the Rev. Carver, our vicar over most of those years, never worked out why we would prefer to climb the vicarage wall for apples, rather than use the gate.

We would cycle miles in small groups into the New Forest; taking packed lunches, and also walk the village footpaths. Forest ponies roamed into the area and were put into pounds at White's Farm, Newton Lane if they strayed towards Brickworth. Gates had to be kept shut always, this was changed and they were fenced back when the new A36 road was built in the early 60's. Wilts and Dorset buses ran between Salisbury and Southampton, from 7.00 am in the morning until midnight, every half-hour most of the day. They were usually full especially when the workers travelled to and from their jobs. A six day return ticket cost 7s.6d. The service to Romsey was less frequent.

The village school had children only up to the age of eleven years, from then one went to the Secondary Modern School at Downton or Grammar Schools in Salisbury. Church and School Fetes were held yearly and the Sunday Schools at the Church and the Methodist Chapel held summer outings to the sea, e.g. Weymouth and Swanage.

Mr Ted Doel and a group of teenagers started a youth Club in 1958. Dr. and Mrs Harding at Abbotstone House allowed us to convert their unused stables into a meeting place. This was really hard work; people in the village gave us spare paint, unwanted furniture, mats, crockery etc. It turned out fine and ended up with a main room and a kitchen area. After completion we spent many happy hours there. We put on plays and pantomimes at the village hall, which were well supported by the village community. Our leader had a boat at Christchurch, which we helped to renovate, making it fit and ready to sail; many weekends were spent at sea. We also enjoyed trips to Speedway, Stockcar Racing and Ice-Skating at Southampton and a few of us even took a trip to Paris for a weekend.

Village dances 'Hops' were regularly held in the village hall in the 60's, always with a live group, these were very popular for miles around.

Television was only just appearing in a few homes in the late 50's. Looking back to this period, we could always provide ourselves with something to do, we were very lucky.

CHAPTER 30

MEMORIES OF MRS ANN ORGAN IN WHITEPARISH

1960 onwards

Ann remembers Mr Hughes the headmaster of the Whiteparish school, as a kind man, much liked, who had a French wife and lived in Common Road where Mr and Mrs Newton, Ann's parents, currently live. He taught the children French to such a high standard that the Secondary Head teacher called in the six or so children from Whiteparish to congratulate them all.

Girls were taught needlework so well that they made summer outfits, skirts and tops, for themselves, not very fashionable embroidery on the hems, gingham material etc., but made to fit and could have been worn.

All children went to Downton Secondary School unless they had passed the 11+ examination when they went to either "South Wilts" or "Bishops". They did not go to any Romsey school.

The school bus followed the old A36 road, picking up children en route (as now). On occasions, when the weather was particularly bad, the bus used to go down Newton Lane in the direction of Redlynch to pick up one of the pupils who lived in one of the farms.

Ann Organ left Downton school and went to Salisbury College to train and there obtained a hairdressing apprenticeship, she remembers feeling privileged to receive £16 a week pay.

There were no Brownies or Guides meetings to keep the girls entertained or occupied. There was a youth club that met in the "Lynches" which was quite a busy village centre. Bring and buy sales were held there.

Badminton was played in the Melchet Hall (village hall). The youngsters used to play a game and then sit a the back of the hall to do their homework before their next game was played.

Confirmation classes were held at the vicarage with the Rev Keeley. It was quite a big class. There were a lot of young people in the village, Meadow Court, Green Close and part of Hop Gardens were all reasonably new housing developments with many young families occupying them. Ann remembers that one of the 'games' after confirmation classes was to run home, all the way placing their feet on the 'cats eyes' in the middle of the road trying not to miss any, there was no problem with traffic.

The Rev. Roger Keeley

Dances were very popular and very noisy, but since most people attended them there were no complaints about the noise. The dances were usually organised by John and Margaret Barrow, (John was the village policeman), and not to be missed. The football club was often involved and a dance was always held during Whiteparish Week. The fact that John Barrow was the local policeman made keeping order much easier, people respected his position. The Whiteparish Week dance used to be a fancy dress affair and was particularly popular. On one occasion the vicar and his wife went as Mr and Mrs Quality Street.

Ann and her partner did win quite often There was not a lot of vandalism, but there was certainly mischief. Often the garden gates were swapped around and Sunday mornings were spent putting them back in their correct places.

Young people sometimes amused themselves by telling ghost stories. There was supposed to be a ghost near the 'Lynches', another at the junction of Common and the lane leading to Cowesfield. The ghost in Nunn's Court was claimed to have been seen by many adults and children, in fact it is alleged that during August days dogs will not walk in the area. Ann is sure that her parents home in Common Road had a ghost which she claims she saw several times - the gate would open - a shadow move to the front door - there would be a knock on the door - the dog would freeze, but when the door was opened nothing was there, but the gate was still open.

The children used to play in the chalk pit, where Pain's Fireworks is now, using the chalk as a toboggan run, great fun when the chalk was wet. This was stopped when gypsies moved into the area.

Attending the doctor's surgery at Wisteria House was not a very comfortable exercise. The waiting room had hard benches and visitors had to shuffle along the benches towards the surgery entrance as each person entered. The medicines were dispensed by the doctors themselves and were obtained by knocking at a hatch, which was down two or three steps out of the reception area. The room was always very neat with bottles etc. stacked in rows on shelves all round the walls. Ann thinks it must have been a difficult job to be a doctor, working and living in the same house being, on call 24 hours a day and at the same time bringing up a family.

Mr Ford ran a plant nursery in the Chalk Pit and Ann was quite impressed by the fact that he had a security system, which was an electric beam, which gave a signal when broken.

Mr Roly Chalk ran a haulage business out of Cowesfield Nurseries on the A27. She has memories of icy roads and the problems the huge lorries had in getting into the grounds of the Nurseries, it is assumed that the roads were not salted or gritted in those days.

The Riding Stables were in operation at this period.

Mr and Mrs Noble ran the 'Kings Head' and organised the Harvest Festival Auction, which raised money to give the elderly folk of the village a little gift of money.

There was excitement one day in one of the pubs when someone was stabbed. Dr Claydon was called and dealt with the women , it was not too serious, and the doctor was heard to say "he'll be all right" but the 'he' turned out to be a 'she'.

Buses used to run into Salisbury around every half-hour well into the late evening. There was uproar when the service was cut to once an hour.

CHAPTER 31

CHARITIES

This village is well endowed with Charities; they all, bar one, came into being before 1900. Initially the Church administered the Charities. Prior to the end of the last century Church leaders were really Parish Clerks as well as being spiritual leaders. When County Councils and then Parish Councils came into being a few years before 1885 they began to take over the administration of these social charities. Why this was we are not sure. Maybe the Vicar was glad to be rid of these chores, or perhaps it was felt to be more democratic to let the elected Parish Council attend to these duties. As far as Whiteparish is concerned the task was quite difficult, for accounts of money received had to be kept and audited, then decisions had to be made as to who was to benefit. As there were five charities each defining where the moneys generated were to go, it must have daunted the average person in the village (having only elementary education) who were only too pleased to hand over the problems to a Council consisting of men used to handling money. It must be understood that power in the early part of this century, was in the hands of the big estate owners, in our case Squire Lawrence, Miss Bristow and to some degree Lord Nelson. Economic dependency on the part of the poor and forelock pulling were part of the system.

The five charities, which benefited residents of Whiteparish, are as follows: -

1 - Robert and Mary Gambling Trust. This charity was established in 1894. Its objects were the relief of five poor men and five poor women within the Parish. We have established that two thirds of the investment income of this trust, was destined to provide medical comforts and nourishment to the most deserving poor. We have not been able to find records of how the remaining third of the investment income was used. The income came from rent charges on houses and farms that the trust had invested in over the years.

2 - Sir John Evelyn charity. It is open to question whether this charity was shared with another parish, possibly Dean. The charity was funded from a will set up in 1684 which decreed that a rent charge of £4 per year on Dean Hill farm should be used by the charity.

3 - The Mary Gambling Trust 1894. As with 1 above this trust was funded from rent charges on property owned by the family.

4 - The Eleemosynary Charity of Elizabeth Hitchcock willed in 1722. This charity was willed to provide 10/- per year to 12 folk. (According to the Shorter Oxford English Dictionary Eleemosynary = Alms).

5 - The Amy Catherine Rachel Davies Charity. Although this charity was set up in 1930 it could not be executed until the sister of Amy Davies died in 1970.

It was originally set up to provide an Almshouse in the village but in 1970 the funds available were not enough to build a house and the moneys were passed to the Charity Commissioners.

Parish Council of Winterparish
Charity Receipts.

Date	£	s	d	Signature of Recipient
1925				March Quarter 1925
				Gambling's Recipients
				Five Men 5/6 each per Quarter
13/3/25		5	6	Treble, Charles. W. C. Treble
13/3/25		5	6	Chant Alfred W.S.P. fr. A. Chant
13/3/25		5	6	Savage, Charles. M. J. Noble
13/3/25		5	6	Alford George . Amy E Alford
13/3/25		5	6	Zebedee Thomas. J. Zebedee
				Five Women 5/6 each
25/6 £2		5	6	Trubb Ann ; Newman Martha
13/3/25		5	6	Dyer, Ann. W.S.P for ann Dyer
11/3/25		5	6	Russell, Emma . Emma Russell
13/3/25		5	6	Spare Lavinia Lavinia E Spare
13/3/25		5	6	Thorn Mary. F. Page for Mary Thorn
				Charity Orders
11/3/25		10	0	Light George, Ash Hill S Light
13/3/25		10	0	Golding. Joshua W.S.P fr J. Golding
11/3/25	1	0	0	Light Henry, Coursefield E. E. Light
				Medical Appliance
11/3/25	1	1	6	Do Vivian for John Noble Hayter,
	5	16	6	

a page taken from the Charities Book showing the recipients in March 1925 of distributions from the 'Gamblings Trust'

Other charities also came to the parish but were destined for education and came originally under the Church's wing, the village school being a Church school, until the County Council came on the scene.

Until 1989 the Parish Council administered all these charities, under the watchful eye of the Charity Commissioners. However the money available for distribution from each charity was of no significance at today's prices. This, of course, was not the case back in 1900; 5/- to a man or woman who when working were probably earning only

15/- a week, with no income when ill, was of great value. It is amusing to read what type of medical comforts was bought for pain relief in the early part of this century. A boy was bought a cushion to relieve pain when sitting, no indication of what caused the pain! Another chap had a 'truss' provided; Hernia in those days was a curse to a working man. Nothing was undertaken which did not involve heavy lifting. The Parish Council purchased meat to give to those who had been ill and needed better food to aid recovery. So the relief went on, even bed sheets were purchased once a year so that some 35 people selected could be given one new sheet. The interesting point to note is that £6 10/- was all the money needed to provide sheets for a period of 30 years. Not a great deal of inflation about. A firm in Salisbury was asked year after year to quote for the sheet charity. They had to provide a sample to the Parish Council each year and deliver the goods to the Parish hall on the day of distribution! It must have been very difficult trying to be fair in the way the money or goods were distributed. No doubt the Council got a great deal of feed back if they appeared to favour a particular person. As far as we can find out the gifts were always signed for by the receiptients. If one considers that many folk around 1900 had been born before schools had become universal, it is amazing that no crosses were used to sign

By 1980, it had become apparent that with Social Security and the National Health Service playing such a big part in helping those in need, these charities needed streamlining. The lady who set this in motion was Mrs Saunders, Chairperson of the Parish Council. Rent charges were commuted and with the help of the Charity Commissioners all five trusts were brought together, and the administration was taken out of the hands of the Council. Although the Council no longer administered the trusts they still had the task of appointing the trustees, although these did not have to be members of the Council. From being five charities in 1900 by 1999 they had been turned into one, the 'Whiteparish Charity', and brought up to date in what help can be given and in what is now a completely changed world compared with 100 years ago.

NB Details of the 'Whiteparish Charity' can be obtained from the Charity Commissioners.

CHAPTER 32

SOME BUILDINGS IN WHITEPARISH, PAST AND PRESENT

One hundred years ago the life of the country and village was dominated by the big houses. The land belonged to the few and, in practice, the way of life for those who were employed by the landowners had changed little for hundreds of years. Domestic servants were employed in considerable numbers to run the large multi-roomed houses: hours were long and wages low - examples: -

A Carpenter was employed on an estate similar to the Cowesfield Estate in 1909 at the rate of £1 4s 3d (£1.20) per fortnight and his foreman would receive £2 2s 4d (£2.12p) per fortnight. A painter would receive 16/10 (84p) per fortnight as his wages while a labourer received anything from 8/- (40p) to 17/6d (87p) a fortnight. Indoor staff earned only a few pounds annually, usually paid quarterly, they of course, had their rooms, food and uniforms provided.

Out in the fields, in the absence of machinery and chemicals, many men were needed to tend horses, stack hayricks, weed crops etc.

How was this reflected in Whiteparish?

For a start there were six large houses (mansions) in the locality. One of the oldest, Abbotstone house, lay in the centre of the village. The others were on the outskirts. Brickworth to the west, Broxmore, Cowesfield and Ashmore to the east and New house to the extreme south-west. In addition there were and still are big farmhouses such as Young's Farm and The Lynches which are still occupied.

The 1895 census reveals that a total of 40 people lived in the six large houses, with probably at least double this number living elsewhere in the village, who were dependent on these houses for work. Bearing in mind that there were approximately 700 adults living in the village at that time, it is clear that well over 10% of the village were dependent on these houses for a living.

Four of these houses remain today. Cowesfield House, built in 1767, was demolished in 1949, having been unoccupied since World War 2. The 30 room mansion was formerly the home of Mr W.F. Lawrence (Squire Lawrence), once Postmaster General and MP for the Abercromby division of Liverpool from 1885 until his defeat in 1906 by 199 votes. The Squire was the dominant force in the village, chairing most of the committees and heading most of the donations to 'good' causes. The driveway to the house can still be seen as you leave the village heading for Romsey. Cowesfield

House had its own source of water and on at least one occasion in the early part of this century the Squire sent water into the village in water carts during a period of drought.

Cowesfield House 1939

Broxmore House

Broxmore House was built in 1812 with C H Tatham as architect; materials used were salvaged from the demolished Alderstone Manor House. At the beginning of the century Mrs Varley Rogers was in residence and in common with most of the large houses it was commandeered in the First World War for Military purposes. The crippling death duties after the war precluded large-scale repairs to this and many other houses and after Miss E S Bristow left the house in the 1930's it was demolished.

Abbotstone House built in 1625 was originally called Street Farm and was part of the Eyres estate. It is in the centre of the village and is still occupied.

Abbotstone House 1999

Ashmore House in Dean Lane was built in 1790. It is still in good repair and occupied.

Early picture of Ashmore House

Brickworth House was built in 1605, destroyed by fire in 1860 and rebuilt in its present form. It is still occupied

New House in what was once the estate of Tychebourne Park was built in 1619 and has been in continuous occupation. It is on the south-western boundary of the parish on the road to Redlynch.

There are several large houses of interest. The Lynches is a house that has had a varied history. It has been a home of a wealthy yeoman farmer, a nunnery, a reading room, a boy's club and has now been divided into several homes. Young's farm, a farmhouse built around 1600, White House and Alderstone House are all family homes. Wisteria House now a family home was previously the home and surgery for the family doctors.

White House

The landmark that is always mentioned when Whiteparish is written about is the Pepperbox, formerly known as Eyre's folly, on the brow of the hill between the village and Salisbury. The land around the Pepperbox is now National Trust Land but has always been a popular recreational area. Passers by in cars, motor bikes and bicycles used to take refreshment from a small café on the site, which even after the Second World War was a favourite rendezvous for youngsters from the village. Nowadays the National Trust works with the senior boys and girls from the school. In fact the children have monitored, over several years, the effect on the plants, flowers and grasses that 'freeranging' 'New Forest' ponies have had on the land. The children have also designed the information board that is now in use on the site.

Eyre's 'folly' standing on the top of Pepperbox hill'

CHAPTER 33

WHITEPARISH BUSINESSES

There has been, as one might expect, great changes in business and employment over the past one hundred years. In 1900 farming and brickworks were the businesses which generated most of the work and money in the village. However in common with most areas in Britain at that time work was hard and wages were low. The village carpenter also became the undertaker or certainly the coffin maker and the cobbler kept everyone booted, although in many cases the man of the family repaired the family's boots as best he could. Blacksmiths had a very important part to play; not only shoeing horses, but also repairing and making tools for farms and gardens. A saddler and harness maker was indispensable. Several bakers supplied bread and groceries and the Post Office was the hub of communications having the only 'phone available for instant access to the outside world. The four public houses supplied the other essential food for hard working men, beer. We can find no reference to any of them brewing beer, as deliveries seem to have come from Romsey and Salisbury. Carriers from the village went to these two towns usually on their market days twice a week. Occasionally they took a passenger and brought back goods that had been ordered the week before.

Mr Till, the saddler, in his shop doorway in 'The Street'

Changes began to take place, as bicycles became more numerous. At least one cycle shop started up in the village, repairing and selling cycles. This was at Speedwell House. World War One triggered the new era of motor transport. Mr Bailey began a bus service, probably with a surplus army vehicle. Mr Dear set up a garage on what is now the A36. Petrol was sold and it would seem that this was the only petrol station between Salisbury and Southampton in the early 1920's. A large redundant building can still be seen which is on the original garage location although it is not the original building. Another garage and petrol pump was set in the Street. The Dear family began a haulage business, this was sold in the late 1980's and their last workshop and garage can be seen along Common road. The local bus service was sold to a bus company. In the 1960's the Rudman family was busy building houses in the village and also erecting farm buildings to accommodate the mechanisation that was then going on apace. Mr Rudman retired a few years ago due to ill health, so that now firms outside the parish are undertaking all building of new houses. Up on Pepperbox Hill a chalk quarry was being worked, the chalk being spread on farmland for miles around.

Mr Chant thatching Wayside Cottage in Common Road

Mr Collins working at his trade from Cobblers Cottage in 'The Street'

Mr Loder and his son making hurdles in Broxmore Wood

The brickworks had long gone by the 1970's. Around this time one of the last sites was sold off for £16,000 to Graham Reeves, a large builder's merchants. This has developed into a business which employs a fair number of people and in this year of 1999 has just been sold to another builder's merchants. We understand it is not to be closed down

An aerial view of Graham's Yard mid 1990s, built on what was once one of the village brickworks

The chalk workings at Pepperbox Hill has, over the years, created a very large hole. Biffa, a firm who are in the business of filling the space with unwanted rubbish from far and wide, has now taken over the area.

Another large hole in the village, which was once part of Chalk Pit farm, and must have been worked for chalk over many centuries, was taken over in 1984 by Pain's Fireworks. It has proved an ideal place for their work, manufacturing fireworks and other pyrotechnics. The headquarters of the company is at Ringwood in the New Forest. Soon after they took over the site there was an explosion in the pit, but since the pit was so deep it caused no problems within the village. In 1984 the company had three employees, now it has nineteen full time employees and one hundred and fifty part timers, not all from the village, as the company are now also operating in Dubai and has supplied fireworks to some of the Saudi Arabian Royal family. At one time the pit was used for rifle practice, probably by the Home Guard, old bullets are still being found embedded in the chalk face

Staff of Pain's Fireworks 1998

Wiltshire C. C. at one time used a building within the village; school diners were cooked there. This property was sold in 1977 to a company called Lascars Electronics Ltd., they came from Essex. This company has expanded it's operations, enlarged the buildings, has started another branch in Fordingbridge and have opened an office in the United States of America. In this parish they now employ around 45 people and have created a most attractive building and a pleasant environment in which to work

Lascar's staff receiving award 'Investor in people 1997'

Lascar's establishment - in Whiteparish

The original Garage and petrol pump that was in the Street was sold in 1966, to a young man Mr Bettridge who started a car accident repair business. Since then Mr Bettridge, who works on his own, has rebuilt the establishment and expanded it from a shed to a purpose built workshop with the title 'Bedwin Sprays' At the Brickworth end of the village there is Brickworth garage that has developed from a small workshop with a single petrol pump to a modern service station. It carries out repairs, sells all types of petrol and diesel and sells food and drink. It is situated on the very busy A36. Another business has been established in Common Road. This is a large truck company, involved in moving freight around Britain and the Continent. It is well placed for this purpose being near the ferry ports of Southampton and Portsmouth.

Bedwin Sprays workshop on the A 27

Brickworth Garage on the A 36

Glendale farm on the A36 and Richmond farm on the A27 have established areas given over to light industrial and commercial use. Small firms and individuals rent the premises they need. Merry Hill farm, which for very many years produced mushrooms, has now reduced this operation and some of their released buildings are also rented out to small businesses. The Post Office stores has changed hands in the last two or three years after being run by the same Woodford family for almost the whole century. Mrs Julie Barnes has expanded the range of goods sold in the shop and it is now proving increasingly popular within the village. There used to be another shop towards the West end of the Street, which until a few years ago sold groceries and had an off-licence. It has been a shop almost since the turn of the century selling almost everything from paraffin and candles to hams. Everything has changed now, the present owners, Mr and Mrs Strugnal, gave up selling groceries and hardware and have developed a sign making business 'Dartwest'. The original working area has been extended at the rear of the shop to cope with additional work.

Dartwest sign-writers

Village shop 1999

Until early 1999 the village had four public houses, the Fountain Inn, the Kings Head, the Parish Lantern and the White Hart. The White Hart has closed and is now a private house. The picture on the introduction page shows the 'Kings Head' and the 'Fountain Inns.

Old picture of the 'White Hart' and its surroundings 1890

Mabel Nobel, proprietor of the 'Kings Head', and her husband 'Sach'. 'Sach' was a woodsman and regularly brought his pony into the bar for its pint of ale. A modern picture of the 'Kings Head' is in on the introduction page

The 'Parish Lantern'

The 'Fountain Inn'

On the A36 what was once Newton Farm has changed from farming to become a large bed and breakfast establishment. Further along the A36 towards Landford there is the busy Hillside caravan and camping site. A smaller caravan site is now opened at the back of what was Whites farm. These places were once smallholdings and as their owners gave up farming for economic or other reasons, other uses have been found for the land. Another instance of diversification took place along Common Road where Brympton Riding School is now found. In 1959 Mrs Near took over a smallholding of a barn and two pigsties. She lived in a caravan until the riding school business had become established and later was able to build a bungalow. The business is now thriving with 20 horses on the books and an outdoor school. A similar thing happened to another farm at the back of the Manor House, Street Farm. Here, Mrs Davies is the owner of a large livery and breeding stable. Before this development Mr Dalgety kept a pack of foxhounds there.

Two enthusiastic young horse women at the Brympton riding school

There is also a well-stocked plant nursery, Courtens, on the A27 on the Romsey side of the village opposite the 'Long Pond' one of very few remaining ponds in the village.

Long pond at the turn of the century, looking East

Modern picture of 'Long Pond', looking West.

Within the last five years the village has lost its butchers shop. This was established well before the century began and had slaughtering facilities, although no animals have been killed there for very many years. The shop served people in and around the parish and had been run by The Hammond family for decades. On the death of Mr Hammond the shop was taken over by Mr Hamblyn who retired when the lease of the building ran out. Mr Hamblyn was famous in the district, having won, in 1989, the butcher's National Sausage Competition in Harrogate.

Robert Hamblyn, prize winning butcher (on the right)

Several people run small businesses that are concerned with building work, gardening, carpentry, electrical work, computer repairs, hairdressing etc. which are well advertised in the popular monthly village magazine, the 'Steeple and Street'. Most of the population in the parish of working age, earn their living out of the parish, commuting by car or using the limited 'bus service. Other people have retired into the village because of its convenient position being reasonably near to Salisbury, Romsey and Southampton. It also has good pubs and restaurants and of course, a very modern surgery which employs five doctors, together with nurses and a pharmacy.

We have, no doubt, failed to mention people who are making their living within the village, for this we apologise. However, we very much hope that what we have in print will give future generations and idea of what life was like in the whole of the century 1900 - 2000.

Inside Whiteparish Stores - current proprietor, Mrs Julie Barnes on the left

CHAPTER 34

FIRSTS AND LASTS AND OTHER NOTABLE EVENTS OF THE CENTURY

1st Baptism Kate Alice Alford 7th January 1900

1st Death Harriet Newman (Harestock) 11th January 1900

1st Marriage George Littley (Aged 28 of Clapham London) to Alice Eliza Hayter (Aged 24 of Whiteparish) 2nd June 1900

1st recorded Village Policeman Alfred Foreman Constable in charge 1911

Mains Water Installed 1939

Mains Drainage Installed 1972 - 73

Electricity Available 1940

The Rev. Roger Keeley presenting Mrs Kemish with her Mother's Union 50 year membership award

Gas Available   1987 - 88

Village Hall (Melchet Hall) Built 1928

Mrs Kemish	Received 50 year medal from Mother's Union	February 1974
Mrs Kemish	Received Maundy Money	11th April 1974
Joan Witchell	Received Queen's Silver Jubilee medal	1977

This award was given to Joan for her services to the nursing profession and to the community.

Last Village Policeman John Barrow, transferred from village   May 1992. Received an award in May 1990 from the High Sheriff of Wiltshire for his professionalism and services to the community. He was the only policeman in the County to receive this award

Exceptional Snowfall 15 to 18 inches deep fell in one day.   25th April 1908

Last, and continuing, village Postman Sid Pegrum

P.C. John Barrow at his desk in the police house in Green Close, now a private home

Sid Pegrum, village postman

Mrs Cobern with the younger children in 1999

Mrs Cobern retired in October 1999 after 25 years of service to the school.

Diana & Richard Stevens' "Folly"

Diana & Richard Stevens' "Folly" Carrying on an old tradition this folly was built in the Steven's garden in 1999 to celebrate the millennium.

Last Baptisms   Joshua Jeth Osborn (aged 8), Oliver Samuel Osborn (aged 6) and Conor Max Osborn (4 months), sons of Philip and Jacquie Osborn of 12 Highlands Way.   31st October 1999

Last Marriage   Philip Davies and Emma Bottomley of Silverlea, Romsey Road.   13th November 1999.

Last Death   Sean Brian Cobern (aged 20),   26th December 1999.

STOP PRESS

The last week of the one hundred years in the village has not gone by without drama.

The weather has been at times cold and very wet, flooding land above Doves Lane. There was a tragedy on Boxing Day when a young man was overcome by smoke from a burning television set and died. He was about to celebrate his 21st birthday. That sad news has taken the edge off the millennium celebrations.

The disclosure by Wiltshire County Council that they wish to build a waste site in or near the village has certainly put the population in a fighting mood.

The last day of the year is a Bank Holiday so only essential work is being done including of course, that of Pub landlords!

As this is being written the clock has struck twelve and the century has passed.

CHAPTER 35

WHITEPARISH LIVING UP
TO ITS NAME

Whiteparish has often lived up to its name throughout this century, the earliest reference appears in the Whiteparish & Landford Church monthly 1907. No doubt although we have only one photograph, taken during the severe winter of 1954, the village must also have suffered during the winters of 1947 and 1963. The photographs below are of some of these.

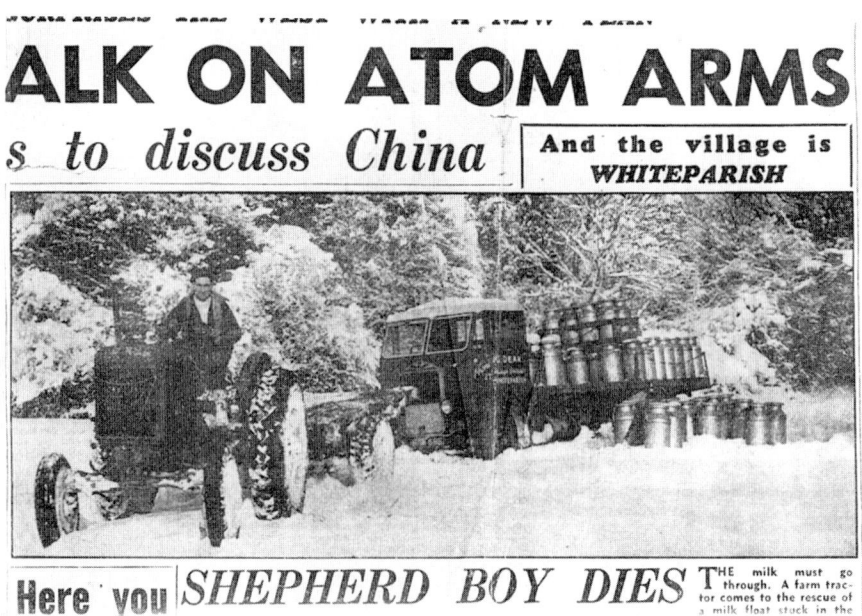

Mr George Dear's milk lorry being towed out of a snowdrift on 29th Jannuary 1954, as reported in the national newspaper the 'News Chronicle'

'The Street' in 1982 following a heavy snowfall'

'The Street' in 1987'

'The Church in 1996'

' The Surgery car park in February 1996'

CHAPTER 36

MODERN HOUSING
DEVELOPMENTS

1960s Ashmore Close

1960s Common Road

1970s The Triangle

1970s Meadow Court

Mid 1980s Croft Heights

1980s Highlands Way

1988 Nunn's Court

Late 1980s The Bramleys

1990s Kingsgate

Highlands Way, Housing Association Houses

1990s A 27 Development

1999 Construction of houses, Martins Rise

1999 Martins Rise

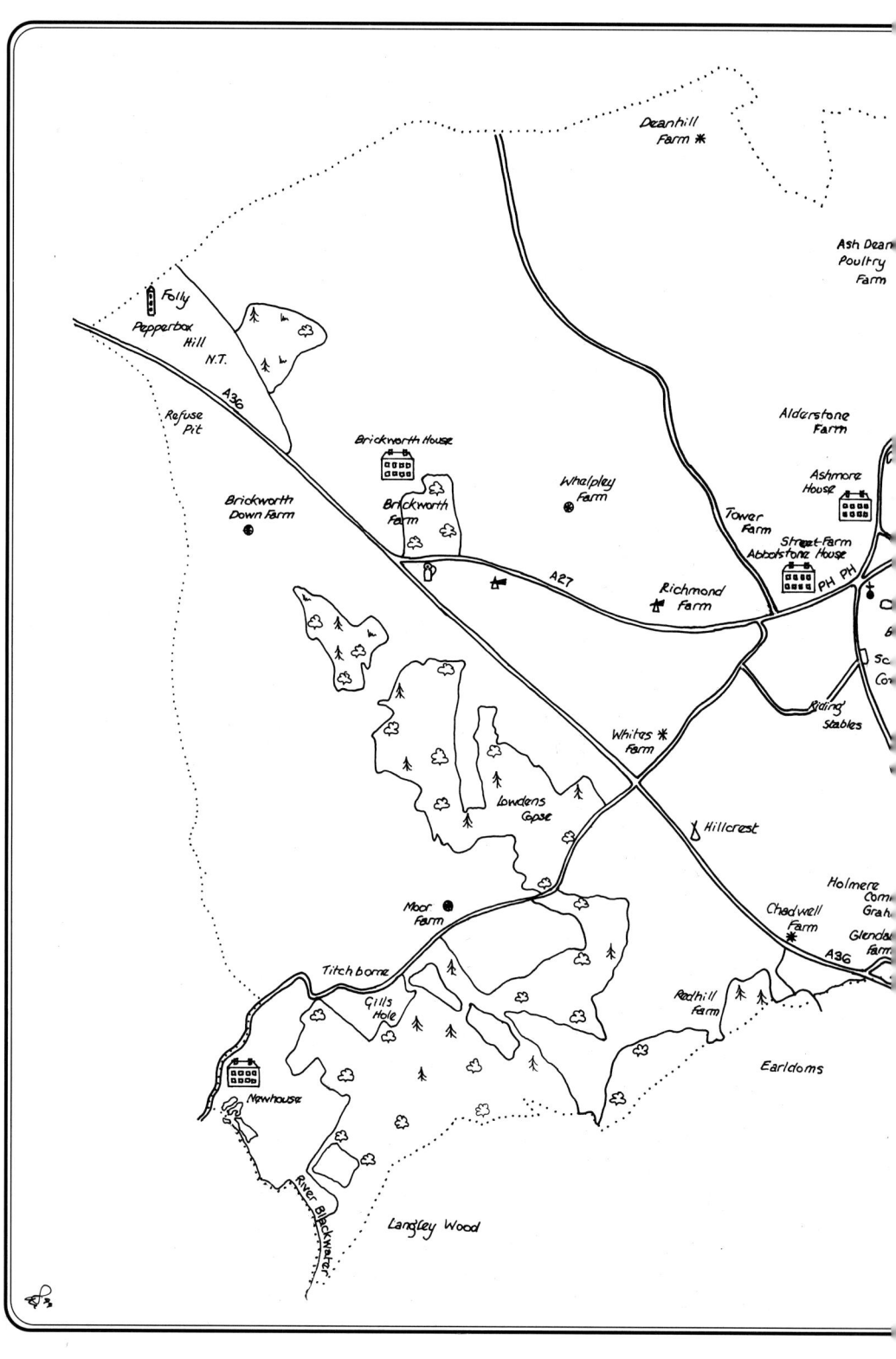

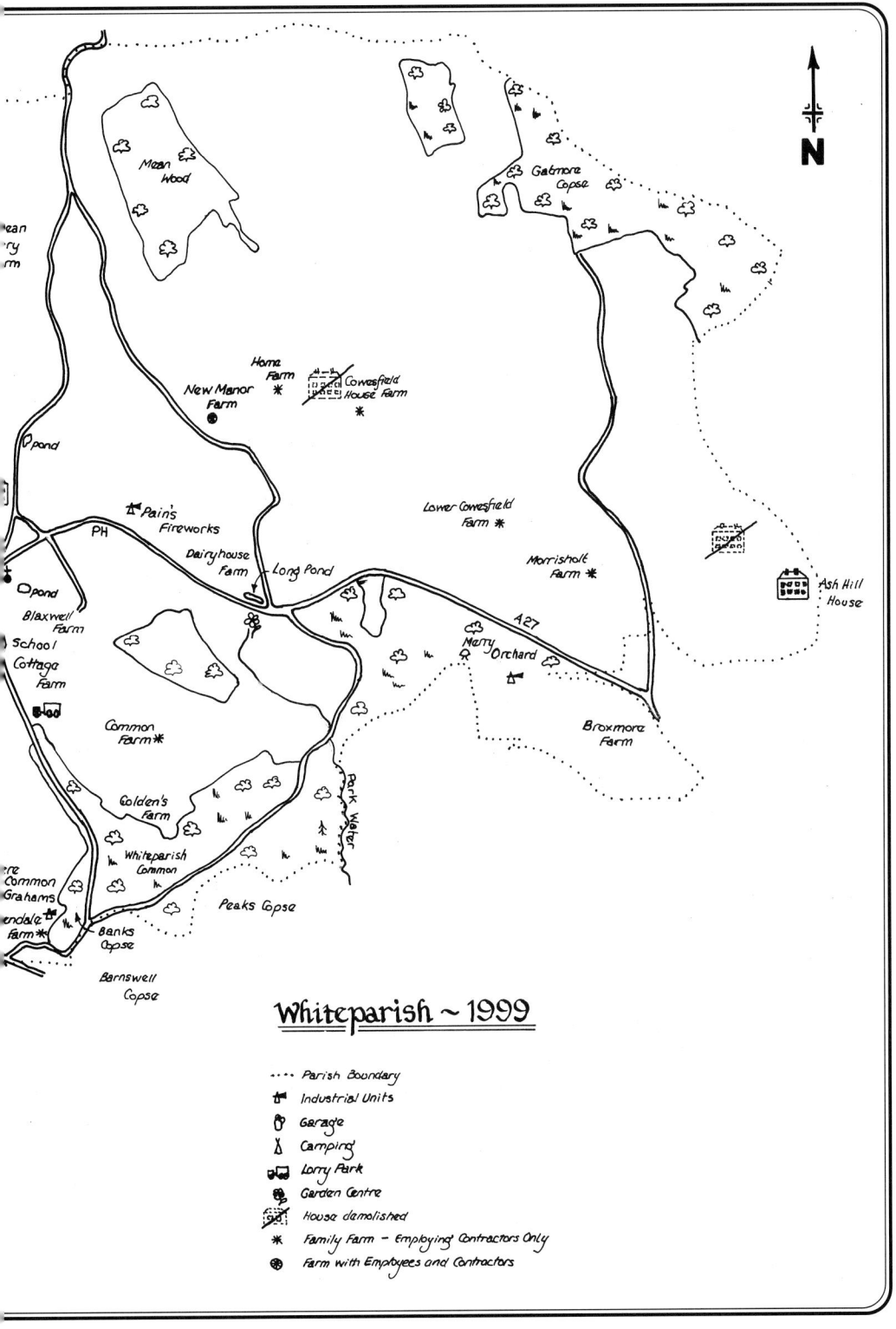

N

Mean
Wood

Gatmore
Copse

Home
Farm
New Manor
Farm

Cowesfield
House Farm

Opond

Pain's
Fireworks

PH

Dairyhouse
Farm

Long Pond

Lower Cowesfield
Farm

Morrisholt
Farm

A27

Ash Hill
House

Opond

Blaxwell
Farm

School
Cottage
Farm

Merry
Orchard

Common
Farm

Broxmore
Farm

Golden's
Farm

Whiteparish
Common

Park Water

Common
Grahams

endale
farm

Banks
Copse

Peaks Copse

Barnswell
Copse

Whiteparish ~ 1999

- - - - Parish Boundary
Industrial Units
Garage
Camping
Lorry Park
Garden Centre
House demolished
✳ Family Farm – Employing Contractors Only
✵ Farm with Employees and Contractors

ACKNOWLEDGEMENTS

To Eric Chase for his idea, nearly two years ago, of putting this book together and to his band of willing helpers, particularly Hugh Burnard, Peter Cook, Paxton King, John Lequesne, Gwyneth Smith and Steve and Juliette Worpole

To our Sponsors Mr P Stone of Quality Lift Products Ltd., Graham Group P L C., Whiteparish Parish Council, Mr J D Atwell, Mrs J Barnes, Mr W J Hedley and Mr P R Sirs.

and to the village members who offered us interest free loans, and in no small measure, enabled us to meet the costs of getting this book printed.

To our contributors, both young and old, for their stories and photographs.

To Julian Fall for proof reading the book.

To Roger Elliott for his professional photographic contributions including both covers of this book

To Dr John Baston for his advice and assistance with the scanning of old photographs.

To the Women's Institute members for allowing copies to be taken of some of the photographs that are in their 'Village Scrap Book'.

To Elizabeth Male for her skilled work in sketching maps of the area.

INDEX